OECD/G20 Base Erosion and Profit Shifting Project

Tax Challenges Arising from Digitalisation of the Economy – Global Anti-Base Erosion Model Rules (Pillar Two)

INCLUSIVE FRAMEWORK ON BEPS

OECD
BETTER POLICIES FOR BETTER LIVES

This document, as well as any data and map included herein, are without prejudice to the status of or sovereignty over any territory, to the delimitation of international frontiers and boundaries and to the name of any territory, city or area.

Please cite this publication as:
OECD (2021), *Tax Challenges Arising from Digitalisation of the Economy – Global Anti-Base Erosion Model Rules (Pillar Two): Inclusive Framework on BEPS*, OECD/G20 Base Erosion and Profit Shifting Project, OECD Publishing, Paris, https://doi.org/10.1787/782bac33-en.

ISBN 978-92-64-72773-1 (print)
ISBN 978-92-64-90268-8 (PDF)

OECD/G20 Base Erosion and Profit Shifting Project
ISSN 2313-2604 (print)
ISSN 2313-2612 (online)

Photo credits: Cover © ninog-Fotolia.com.

Corrigenda to OECD publications may be found at: https://www.oecd.org/en/publications/support/corrigenda.html.

Foreword

Digitalisation and globalisation have had a profound impact on economies and the lives of people around the world, and this impact has only accelerated in the 21st century. These changes have brought with them challenges to the rules for taxing international business income, which have prevailed for more than a hundred years and created opportunities for base erosion and profit shifting (BEPS), requiring bold moves by policy makers to restore confidence in the system and ensure that profits are taxed where economic activities take place and value is created.

In 2013, the OECD ramped up efforts to address these challenges in response to growing public and political concerns about tax avoidance by large multinationals. The OECD and G20 countries joined forces and developed an Action Plan to address BEPS in September 2013. The Action Plan identified 15 actions aimed at introducing coherence in the domestic rules that affect cross-border activities, reinforcing substance requirements in the existing international standards, and improving transparency as well as certainty.

After two years of work, measures in response to the 15 actions, including those published in an interim form in 2014, were consolidated into a comprehensive package and delivered to G20 Leaders in November 2015. The BEPS package represents the first substantial renovation of the international tax rules in almost a century. As the BEPS measures are implemented, it is expected that profits will be reported where the economic activities that generate them are carried out and where value is created. BEPS planning strategies that rely on outdated rules or on poorly co-ordinated domestic measures will be rendered ineffective.

OECD and G20 countries also agreed to continue to work together to ensure a consistent and co ordinated implementation of the BEPS recommendations and to make the project more inclusive. As a result, they created the OECD/G20 Inclusive Framework on BEPS (Inclusive Framework), bringing all interested and committed countries and jurisdictions on an equal footing in the Committee on Fiscal Affairs and its subsidiary bodies. With over 140 members, the Inclusive Framework monitors and peer reviews the implementation of the minimum standards and is completing the work on standard setting to address BEPS issues. In addition to its members, other international organisations and regional tax bodies are involved in the work of the Inclusive Framework, which also consults business and the civil society on its different work streams.

Although implementation of the BEPS package is dramatically changing the international tax landscape and improving the fairness of tax systems, one of the key outstanding BEPS issues – to address the tax challenges arising from the digitalisation of the economy – remained unresolved. In a major step forward on 8 October 2021, over 135 Inclusive Framework members, representing more than 95% of global GDP, joined a two-pillar solution to reform the international taxation rules and ensure that multinational enterprises pay a fair share of tax wherever they operate and generate profits in today's digitalised and globalised world economy. The implementation of these new rules is envisaged by 2023.

This report was approved by the Inclusive Framework on 14 December 2021 and prepared for publication by the OECD Secretariat.

Table of contents

Abbreviations and acronyms

CE	Constituent Entity
ETR	Effective Tax Rate
GloBE	Global Anti-Base Erosion
IFRS	International Financial Reporting Standards
JV	Joint Venture
MNE	Multinational enterprise
OECD	Organisation for Economic Co-operation and Development
UPE	Ultimate Parent Entity

Executive summary

The Global Anti-Base Erosion (GloBE) Rules provide for a co-ordinated system of taxation intended to ensure large multinational enterprise (MNE) groups pay a minimum level of tax on the income arising in each of the jurisdictions where they operate. It does so by imposing a top-up tax on profits arising in a jurisdiction whenever the effective tax rate, determined on a jurisdictional basis, is below the minimum rate.

- Chapter 1 defines the scope of the GloBE Rules.
- Chapter 2 determines the constituent entities in the group that are liable for any top-up tax and the portion of any top-up tax charged to any such entity.
- Chapters 3 and 4 set out the components of the effective tax rate calculation under the GloBE Rules. Chapter 3 determines the income (or loss) for the period for each constituent entity in the MNE Group and Chapter 4 then identifies the taxes attributable to such income
- Chapter 5 aggregates the income and taxes of all constituent entities located in the same jurisdiction to determine the effective tax rate for that jurisdiction. If the effective tax rate is below the minimum rate, the difference results in a top-up tax percentage which is applied to the jurisdictional income to determine the total amount of top-up tax. The top-up tax is pro-rated amongst the constituent entities located in that jurisdiction and then charged to the constituent entities liable for any top-up tax in accordance with Chapter 2. Chapter 5 also includes an elective substance-based income exclusion that may reduce the amount of profits subject to any top-up tax.
- Chapter 6 contains rules relating to acquisitions, disposals and joint ventures.
- Chapter 7 deals with the application of the GloBE Rules to certain tax neutrality and other distribution regimes.
- Chapter 8 covers administrative aspects of the GloBE Rules including information filing requirements as well as the application of any safe-harbours.
- Chapter 9 sets out certain transitional rules.
- Chapter 10 sets out defined terms used in the GloBE Rules.

The GloBE Rules apply a minimum rate on a jurisdictional basis. In that context, the OECD/G20 Inclusive Framework on BEPS agreed, in its 8 October 2021 statement, that consideration will be given to the conditions under which the US Global Intangible Low-Taxed Income (GILTI) regime will co-exist with the GloBE Rules, to ensure a level playing field.

1 Scope

Operation of the rules in this chapter

Chapter 1 defines the scope of the rules.

- Article 1.1 determines which MNE Groups and Group Entities are subject to the GloBE Rules.
- Article 1.2 to Article 1.4 set out a number of key definitions that are used to determine when an Entity or collection of Entities constitutes a Group and when that Group qualifies as an MNE Group.
- Article 1.5 specifies those Entities that are Excluded Entities and therefore outside the operative provisions of the GloBE Rules.

Article 1.1. Scope of GloBE Rules

1.1.1. The GloBE Rules apply to Constituent Entities that are members of an MNE Group that has annual revenue of EUR 750 million or more in the Consolidated Financial Statements of the Ultimate Parent Entity (UPE) in at least two of the four Fiscal Years immediately preceding the tested Fiscal Year. Further rules are set out in Article 6.1 which modify the application of the consolidated revenue threshold in certain cases.

1.1.2. If one or more of the Fiscal Years of the MNE Group taken into account for purposes of Article 1.1.1 is of a period other than 12 months, for each of those Fiscal Years the EUR 750 million threshold is adjusted proportionally to correspond with the length of the relevant Fiscal Year.

1.1.3. Entities that are Excluded Entities are not subject to the GloBE Rules.

Article 1.2. MNE Group and Group

1.2.1. An MNE Group means any Group that includes at least one Entity or Permanent Establishment that is not located in the jurisdiction of the Ultimate Parent Entity.

1.2.2. A Group means a collection of Entities that are related through ownership or control such that the assets, liabilities, income, expenses and cash flows of those Entities:

(a) are included in the Consolidated Financial Statements of the Ultimate Parent Entity; or

(b) are excluded from the Consolidated Financial Statements of the Ultimate Parent Entity solely on size or materiality grounds, or on the grounds that the Entity is held for sale.

1.2.3. A Group also means an Entity that is located in one jurisdiction and has one or more Permanent Establishments located in other jurisdictions provided that the Entity is not a part of another Group described in Article 1.2.2.

Article 1.3. Constituent Entity

1.3.1. A Constituent Entity is:

(a) any Entity that is included in a Group; and

(b) any Permanent Establishment of a Main Entity that is within paragraph (a).

1.3.2. A Permanent Establishment that is a Constituent Entity under paragraph (b) above shall be treated as separate from the Main Entity and any other Permanent Establishment of that Main Entity.

1.3.3. A Constituent Entity does not include an Entity that is an Excluded Entity.

Article 1.4. Ultimate Parent Entity

1.4.1. Ultimate Parent Entity means either:

(a) an Entity that:

i. owns directly or indirectly a Controlling Interest in any other Entity; and

ii. is not owned, with a Controlling Interest, directly or indirectly by another Entity; or

(b) the Main Entity of a Group that is within Article 1.2.3.

Article 1.5. Excluded Entity

1.5.1. An Excluded Entity is an Entity that is:

(a) a Governmental Entity;

(b) an International Organisation;

(c) a Non-profit Organisation;

(d) a Pension Fund;

(e) an Investment Fund that is an Ultimate Parent Entity; or

(f) a Real Estate Investment Vehicle that is an Ultimate Parent Entity.

1.5.2. An Excluded Entity is also an Entity:

(a) where at least 95% of the value of the Entity is owned (directly or through a chain of Excluded Entities) by one or more Excluded Entities referred to in Article 1.5.1 (other than a Pension Services Entity) and where that Entity:

i. operates exclusively or almost exclusively to hold assets or invest funds for the benefit of the Excluded Entity or Entities; or

ii. only carries out activities that are ancillary to those carried out by the Excluded Entity or Entities; or

(b) where at least 85% of the value of the Entity is owned (directly or through a chain of Excluded Entities), by one or more Excluded Entities referred to in Article 1.5.1 (other than a Pension Services Entity) provided that substantially all of the Entity's income is Excluded Dividends or Excluded Equity Gain or Loss that is excluded from the computation of GloBE Income or Loss in accordance with Articles 3.2.1(b) or (c).

1.5.3. A Filing Constituent Entity may elect not to treat an Entity as an Excluded Entity under Article 1.5.2. An election under this Article is a Five-Year Election.

2 Charging Provisions

Operation of the rules in this chapter

Under this chapter, the amount of Top-Up Tax charged to a Parent Entity or to the Constituent Entities located in a UTPR Jurisdiction is determined:

- by attributing the Top-Up Tax of each Low-Taxed Constituent Entity determined under the rules in Chapter 5 to the Parent Entity under the IIR in accordance with Article 2.1 to Article 2.3; and then
- by allocating the residual Top-Up Tax, if any, to UTPR Jurisdictions in accordance with Article 2.4 to Article 2.6.

Article 2.1. Application of the IIR

2.1.1. A Constituent Entity, that is the Ultimate Parent Entity of an MNE Group, located in [insert name of implementing-jurisdiction] that owns (directly or indirectly) an Ownership Interest in a Low-Taxed Constituent Entity at any time during the Fiscal Year shall pay a tax in an amount equal to its Allocable Share of the Top-Up Tax of that Low-Taxed Constituent Entity for the Fiscal Year.

2.1.2. An Intermediate Parent Entity of an MNE Group located in [insert name of implementing-jurisdiction] that owns (directly or indirectly) an Ownership Interest in a Low-Taxed Constituent Entity at any time during a Fiscal Year shall pay a tax in an amount equal to its Allocable Share of the Top-Up Tax of that Low-Taxed Constituent Entity for the Fiscal Year.

2.1.3. Article 2.1.2 shall not apply if:

(a) the Ultimate Parent Entity of the MNE Group is required to apply a Qualified IIR for that Fiscal Year; or

(b) another Intermediate Parent Entity that owns (directly or indirectly) a Controlling Interest in the Intermediate Parent Entity is required to apply a Qualified IIR for that Fiscal Year.

2.1.4. Notwithstanding Articles 2.1.1 to 2.1.3, a Partially-Owned Parent Entity located in [insert name of implementing-jurisdiction] that owns (directly or indirectly) an Ownership Interest in a Low-Taxed Constituent Entity at any time during the Fiscal Year shall pay a tax in an amount equal to its Allocable Share of the Top-up Tax of that Low-Taxed Constituent Entity for the Fiscal Year.

2.1.5. Article 2.1.4 shall not apply if the Partially-Owned Parent Entity is wholly owned (directly or indirectly) by another Partially-Owned Parent Entity that is required to apply a Qualified IIR for that Fiscal Year.

2.1.6. A Parent Entity located in [insert name of implementing-jurisdiction] shall apply the provisions of Articles 2.1.1 to 2.1.5 with respect to a Low-Taxed Constituent Entity that is not located in [insert name of implementing-jurisdiction].

Article 2.2. Allocation of Top-Up Tax under the IIR

2.2.1. A Parent Entity's Allocable Share of the Top-up Tax of a Low-Taxed Constituent Entity is an amount equal to the Top-up Tax of the Low-Taxed Constituent Entity as calculated under Chapter 5 multiplied by the Parent Entity's Inclusion Ratio for the Low-Taxed Constituent Entity for the Fiscal Year.

2.2.2. A Parent Entity's Inclusion Ratio for a Low-Taxed Constituent Entity for a Fiscal Year is the ratio of (a) the GloBE Income of the Low-Taxed Constituent Entity for the Fiscal Year, reduced by the amount of such income attributable to Ownership Interests held by other owners, to (b) the GloBE Income of the Low-Taxed Constituent Entity for the Fiscal Year.

2.2.3. The amount of GloBE Income attributable to Ownership Interests in a Low-Taxed Constituent Entity held by other owners is the amount that would have been treated as attributable to such owners under the principles of the Acceptable Financial Accounting Standard used in the Ultimate Parent Entity's Consolidated Financial Statements if the Low-Taxed Constituent Entity's net income were equal to its GloBE Income and:

(a) the Parent Entity had prepared Consolidated Financial Statements in accordance with that accounting standard (the hypothetical Consolidated Financial Statements);

(b) the Parent Entity owned a Controlling Interest in the Low-Taxed Constituent Entity such that all of the income and expenses of the Low-Taxed Constituent Entity were consolidated on a line-by-line basis with those of the Parent Entity in the hypothetical Consolidated Financial Statements;

(c) all of the Low-Taxed Constituent Entity's GloBE Income were attributable to transactions with persons that are not Group Entities; and

(d) all Ownership Interests not directly or indirectly held by the Parent Entity were held by persons other than Group Entities.

2.2.4. In the case of a Flow-through Entity, GloBE Income under this Article shall not include any income allocated, pursuant to Article 3.5.3, to an owner that is not a Group Entity.

Article 2.3. IIR Offset Mechanism

2.3.1. A Parent Entity that owns an Ownership Interest in a Low-Taxed Constituent Entity indirectly through an Intermediate Parent Entity or a Partially-Owned Parent Entity that is not eligible for an exclusion from the IIR under Article 2.1.3 or 2.1.5 shall reduce its allocable share of a Top-up Tax of the Low-Taxed Constituent Entity in accordance with Article 2.3.2.

2.3.2. The reduction in Article 2.3.1 will be an amount equal to the portion of the Parent Entity's Allocable Share of the Top-up Tax that is brought into charge by the Intermediate Parent Entity or the Partially-Owned Parent Entity under a Qualified IIR.

Article 2.4. Application of the UTPR

2.4.1. Constituent Entities of an MNE Group located in [insert name of implementing-Jurisdiction] shall be denied a deduction (or required to make an equivalent adjustment under domestic law) in an amount resulting in those Constituent Entities having an additional cash tax expense equal to the UTPR Top-up Tax Amount for the Fiscal Year allocated to that jurisdiction.

2.4.2. The adjustment mentioned in Article 2.4.1 shall apply to the extent possible with respect to the taxable year in which the Fiscal Year ends. If this adjustment is insufficient to produce an additional cash tax expense for this taxable year equal to the UTPR Top-up Tax Amount allocated to [insert name of implementing-Jurisdiction] for the Fiscal Year, the difference shall be carried forward to the extent necessary to the succeeding Fiscal Years and be subject to the adjustment mentioned in Article 2.4.1 to the extent possible for each taxable year.

2.4.3. Article 2.4.1 shall not apply to a Constituent Entity that is an Investment Entity.

Article 2.5. UTPR Top-up Tax Amount

2.5.1. The Total UTPR Top-up Tax Amount for a Fiscal Year shall be equal to the sum of the Top-up Tax calculated for each Low-Taxed Constituent Entity of an MNE Group for that Fiscal Year (determined in accordance with Article 5.2), subject to the adjustments set out in this Article 2.5 and Article 9.3.

2.5.2. The Top-up Tax calculated for a Low-Taxed Constituent Entity that is otherwise taken into account under Article 2.5.1 shall be reduced to zero if all of the Ultimate Parent Entity's Ownership Interests in such Low-Taxed Constituent Entity are held directly or indirectly by one or more Parent Entities that are required to apply a Qualified IIR in the jurisdiction where they are located with respect to that Low-Taxed Constituent Entity for the Fiscal Year.

2.5.3. Where Article 2.5.2 does not apply, the Top-up Tax calculated for a Low-Taxed Constituent Entity that is otherwise taken into account under Article 2.5.1 shall be reduced by a Parent Entity's Allocable Share of the Top-up Tax of that Low-Taxed Constituent Entity that is brought into charge under a Qualified IIR.

Article 2.6. Allocation of Top-Up Tax for the UTPR

2.6.1. Subject to Articles 2.6.2 and 2.6.3, the UTPR Top-up Tax Amount allocated to [insert name of implementing-Jurisdiction] shall be determined by multiplying the Total UTPR Top-up Tax Amount determined in Article 2.5.1 by the jurisdiction's UTPR Percentage. The UTPR Percentage of [insert name of implementing-Jurisdiction] shall be determined each Fiscal Year for each MNE Group as follows:

$$50\% \text{ x } \frac{\textit{Number of Employees in the jurisdiction}}{\textit{Number of Employees in all UTPR jurisdictions}} + 50\% \text{ x } \frac{\textit{Total value of Tangible Assets in the jurisdiction}}{\textit{Total value of Tangible Assets in all UTPR jurisdictions}}$$

Where, for each Fiscal Year:

(a) the Number of Employees in the jurisdiction is the total Number of Employees of all the Constituent Entities of the MNE Group located in [insert name of implementing-Jurisdiction];

(b) the Number of Employees in all UTPR Jurisdictions is the total Number of Employees of all the Constituent Entities of the MNE Group located in a jurisdiction that has a Qualified UTPR in force for the Fiscal Year;

(c) the total value of Tangible Assets in the jurisdiction is the sum of the Net Book Values of Tangible Assets of all the Constituent Entities of the MNE Group located in [insert name of implementing-Jurisdiction];

(d) the total value of Tangible Assets in all UTPR Jurisdictions is the sum of the Net Book Values of Tangible Assets of all the Constituent Entities of the MNE Group located in a jurisdiction that has a Qualified UTPR in Force for the Fiscal Year.

2.6.2. For purposes of Article 2.6.1,

(a) the Number of Employees employed and the Net Book Value of Tangible Assets held by an Investment Entity shall be excluded from the elements of the formula for allocating the Total UTPR Top-up Tax Amount;

(b) the Number of Employees employed and the Net Book Value of Tangible Assets held by a Flow-through Entity that are not allocated to Permanent Establishments shall be allocated to the Constituent Entities (if any) that are located in the jurisdiction where the Flow-through Entity was created. The Number of Employees employed and the Net Book Value of Tangible Assets held by a Flow-through Entity that are not allocated either to Permanent Establishments or under this provision shall be excluded from the formula for allocating the Total UTPR Top-up Tax Amount.

2.6.3. Notwithstanding Article 2.6.1, the UTPR Percentage of [insert name of implementing-Jurisdiction] for an MNE Group is deemed to be zero for a Fiscal Year as long as the Top-Up Tax Amount allocated to [insert name of implementing-Jurisdiction] in a prior Fiscal Year has not resulted in the Constituent Entities of this MNE Group located in [insert name of implementing-Jurisdiction] having an additional cash tax expense equal, in total, to the UTPR Top-up Tax Amount for that prior Fiscal Year allocated to [insert name of implementing-Jurisdiction]. The Number of Employees and the Tangible Assets of the Constituent Entities of this MNE Group located in a jurisdiction with a UTPR Percentage of zero for a Fiscal Year shall be excluded from the formula provided under Article 2.6.1 for allocating the Total UTPR Top-up Tax Amount for that Fiscal Year.

2.6.4. Article 2.6.3 does not apply for a Fiscal Year if all jurisdictions with a Qualified UTPR in Force for the Fiscal Year have a UTPR Percentage of zero for the MNE Group for that Fiscal Year.

3 Computation of GloBE Income or Loss

Operation of the rules in this chapter

Under this chapter, the amount of GloBE Income or Loss of a Constituent Entity is determined:

- by taking the Financial Accounting Net Income or Loss determined for the Constituent Entity for the Fiscal Year in accordance with Article 3.1; and then
- by adjusting this amount under Article 3.2 to Article 3.5 to arrive at that Entity's GloBE Income or Loss.

Article 3.1. Financial Accounts

3.1.1. The GloBE Income or Loss of each Constituent Entity is the Financial Accounting Net Income or Loss determined for the Constituent Entity for the Fiscal Year adjusted for the items described in Article 3.2 to Article 3.5.

3.1.2. Financial Accounting Net Income or Loss is the net income or loss determined for a Constituent Entity (before any consolidation adjustments eliminating intra-group transactions) in preparing Consolidated Financial Statements of the Ultimate Parent Entity.

3.1.3. If it is not reasonably practicable to determine the Financial Accounting Net Income or Loss for a Constituent Entity based on the accounting standard used in the preparation of Consolidated Financial Statements of the Ultimate Parent Entity, the Financial Accounting Net Income or Loss for the Constituent Entity for the Fiscal Year may be determined using another Acceptable Financial Accounting Standard or an Authorised Financial Accounting Standard if:

(a) the financial accounts of the Constituent Entity are maintained based on that accounting standard;

(b) the information contained in the financial accounts is reliable; and

(c) permanent differences in excess of EUR 1 million that arise from the application of a particular principle or standard to items of income or expense or transactions that differs from the financial standard used in the preparation of the Consolidated Financial Statements of the Ultimate Parent Entity are conformed to the treatment required under the accounting standard used in the Consolidated Financial Statements of the Ultimate Parent Entity.

Article 3.2. Adjustments to determine GloBE Income or Loss

3.2.1. A Constituent Entity's Financial Accounting Net Income or Loss is adjusted for the following items to arrive at that Entity's GloBE Income or Loss:

(a) Net Taxes Expense;

(b) Excluded Dividends;

(c) Excluded Equity Gain or Loss;

(d) Included Revaluation Method Gain or Loss;

(e) Gain or loss from disposition of assets and liabilities excluded under Article 6.3;

(f) Asymmetric Foreign Currency Gains or Losses;

(g) Policy Disallowed Expenses;

(h) Prior Period Errors and Changes in Accounting Principles; and

(i) Accrued Pension Expense.

3.2.2. At the election of the Filing Constituent Entity, a Constituent Entity may substitute the amount allowed as a deduction in the computation of its taxable income in its location for the amount expensed in its financial accounts for a cost or expense of such Constituent Entity that was paid with stock-based compensation. If the stock-based compensation expense arises in connection with an option that expires without exercise, the Constituent Entity must include the total amount previously deducted in the computation of its GloBE Income or Loss for the Fiscal Year in which the option expires. The election is a Five-Year Election and must be applied consistently to the stock-based compensation of all Constituent Entities located in the same jurisdiction for the year in which the election is made and all subsequent Fiscal Years. If the election is made in a Fiscal Year after some of the stock-based compensation of a transaction has been recorded in the financial accounts, the Constituent Entity must include in the computation of its GloBE Income or Loss for that Fiscal Year an amount equal to the excess of the cumulative amount allowed as an expense in the computation of its GloBE Income or Loss in previous Fiscal Years over the cumulative amount that would have been allowed as an expense if the election had been in place in those Fiscal Years. If the election is revoked, the Constituent Entity must include in the computation of its GloBE Income or Loss for the revocation year the amount deducted pursuant to the election that exceeds financial accounting expense accrued in respect of the stock-based compensation that has not been paid.

3.2.3. Any transaction between Constituent Entities located in different jurisdictions that is not recorded in the same amount in the financial accounts of both Constituent Entities or that is not consistent with the Arm's Length Principle must be adjusted so as to be in the same amount and consistent with the Arm's Length Principle. A loss from a sale or other transfer of an asset between two Constituent Entities located in the same jurisdiction that is not recorded consistent with the Arm's Length Principle shall be recomputed based on the Arm's Length Principle if that loss is included in the computation of GloBE Income or Loss. Rules for allocating income or loss between a Main Entity and its Permanent Establishments are found in Article 3.4.

3.2.4. Qualified Refundable Tax Credits shall be treated as income in the computation of GloBE Income or Loss of a Constituent Entity. Non-Qualified Refundable Tax Credits shall not be treated as income in the computation of GloBE Income or Loss of a Constituent Entity.

3.2.5. With respect to assets and liabilities that are subject to fair value or impairment accounting in the Consolidated Financial Statements, a Filing Constituent Entity may elect to determine gains and losses using the realisation principle for purposes of computing GloBE Income. The election is a Five-Year Election and applies to all Constituent Entities located in the jurisdiction to which the election applies. The election applies to all assets and liabilities of such Constituent Entities, unless the Filing Constituent Entity chooses to limit the election to tangible assets of such Constituent Entities or to Constituent Entities that are Investment Entities. Under this election:

(a) all gains or losses attributable to fair value or impairment accounting with respect to an asset or liability shall be excluded from the computation of GloBE Income or Loss;

(b) the carrying value of an asset or liability for purposes of determining gain or loss shall be its carrying value at the later of:

(i) the first day of the election year, or

(ii) the date the asset was acquired or liability was incurred; and

(c) if the election is revoked, the GloBE Income or Loss of the Constituent Entities is adjusted by the difference at the beginning of the revocation year between the fair value of the asset or liability and the carrying value of the asset or liability determined pursuant to the election.

3.2.6. Where there is Aggregate Asset Gain in a jurisdiction in a Fiscal Year, the Filing Constituent Entity may make, under this Article 3.2.6, an Annual Election for that jurisdiction to adjust GloBE Income or Loss with respect to each previous Fiscal Year in the Look-back Period in the manner described in paragraphs (b) and (c) and to spread any remaining Adjusted Asset Gain over the Look-back Period in the manner described in paragraph (d). The Effective Tax Rate (ETR) and Top-up Tax, if any, for any previous Fiscal Year must be re-calculated under Article 5.4.1. When an election is made under this Article:

(a) Covered Taxes with respect to any Net Asset Gain or Net Asset Loss in the Election Year shall be excluded from the computation of Adjusted Covered Taxes.

(b) The Aggregate Asset Gain in the Election Year shall be carried-back to the earliest Loss Year and set-off ratably against any Net Asset Loss of any Constituent Entity located in that jurisdiction.

(c) If, for any Loss Year, the Adjusted Asset Gain exceeds the total amount of Net Asset Loss of all Constituent Entities located in that jurisdiction, the Adjusted Asset Gain shall be carried forward to the following Loss Year (if any) and applied ratably against any Net Asset Loss of any Constituent Entity located in that jurisdiction.

(d) Any Adjusted Asset Gain that remains after the application of paragraphs (b) and (c) shall be allocated evenly to each Fiscal Year in the Look-back Period. The Allocated Asset Gain for the relevant year shall be included in the computation of GloBE Income or Loss for a Constituent Entity located in that jurisdiction in that year in accordance with the following formula:

$$\mathit{Allocated\ Asset\ Gain\ for\ relevant\ year} \times \frac{\mathit{The\ specified\ Constituent\ Entity's\ Net\ Asset\ Gain\ in\ the\ Election\ Year}}{\mathit{The\ Net\ Asset\ Gain\ of\ all\ specified\ Constituent\ Entities\ in\ the\ Election\ Year}}$$

For the purposes of the above formula, a specified Constituent Entity is Constituent Entity that has Net Asset Gain in the Election Year and was located in the jurisdiction in the relevant year. If there is no specified Constituent Entity for a relevant year the Adjusted Asset Gain allocated to that year will be allocated equally to each Constituent Entity in the jurisdiction in that year.

3.2.7. The computation of a Low-Tax Entity's GloBE Income or Loss shall exclude any expense attributable to an Intragroup Financing Arrangement that can reasonably be anticipated, over the expected duration of the arrangement to:

(a) increase the amount of expenses taken into account in calculating the GloBE Income or Loss of the Low-Tax Entity;

(b) without resulting in a commensurate increase in the taxable income of the High-Tax Counterparty.

3.2.8. An Ultimate Parent Entity may elect to apply its consolidated accounting treatment to eliminate income, expense, gains, and losses from transactions between Constituent Entities that are located, and included in a tax consolidation group, in the same jurisdiction for purposes of computing each such Constituent Entity's Net GloBE Income or Loss. The election under this Article is a Five-Year Election. Upon making or revoking such election, appropriate adjustments shall be made for GloBE purposes such that there shall not be duplications or omissions of items of GloBE Income or Loss as a result of having made or revoked the election.

3.2.9. An insurance company shall exclude from the computation of GloBE Income or Loss amounts charged to policyholders for Taxes paid by the insurance company in respect of returns to the policy holders. An insurance company shall include in the computation of GloBE Income or Loss any returns to policyholders that are not reflected in Financial Accounting Net Income or Loss to the extent the corresponding increase or decrease in liability to the policyholders is reflected in its Financial Accounting Net Income or Loss.

3.2.10. Amounts recognised as a decrease to the equity of a Constituent Entity attributable to distributions paid or payable in respect of Additional Tier One Capital issued by the Constituent Entity shall be treated as an expense in the computation of its GloBE Income or Loss. Amounts recognised as an increase to the equity of a Constituent Entity attributable to distributions received or receivable in respect of Additional Tier One Capital held by the Constituent Entity shall be included in the computation of its GloBE Income or Loss.

3.2.11. A Constituent Entity's Financial Accounting Net Income or Loss must be adjusted as necessary to reflect the requirements of the relevant provisions of Chapters 6 and 7.

Article 3.3. International Shipping Income exclusion

3.3.1. For an MNE Group that has International Shipping Income, each Constituent Entity's International Shipping Income and Qualified Ancillary International Shipping Income shall be excluded from the computation of its GloBE Income or Loss under Article 3.2 for the jurisdiction in which it is located. Where the computation of a Constituent Entity's International Shipping Income and Qualified Ancillary International Shipping Income results in a loss, the loss shall be excluded from the computation of its GloBE Income or Loss.

3.3.2. International Shipping Income means the net income obtained by a Constituent Entity from:

(a) the transportation of passengers or cargo by ships that it operates in international traffic, whether the ship is owned, leased or otherwise at the disposal of the Constituent Entity;

(b) the transportation of passengers or cargo by ships operated in international traffic under slot-chartering arrangements;

(c) leasing a ship, to be used for the transportation of passengers or cargo in international traffic, on charter fully equipped, crewed and supplied;

(d) leasing a ship on a bare boat charter basis, for the use of transportation of passengers or cargo in international traffic, to another Constituent Entity;

(e) the participation in a pool, a joint business or an international operating agency for the transportation of passengers or cargo by ships in international traffic; and

(f) the sale of a ship used for the transportation of passengers or cargo in international traffic provided that the ship has been held for use by the Constituent Entity for a minimum of one year.

International Shipping Income shall not include net income obtained from the transportation of passengers or cargo by ships via inland waterways within the same jurisdiction.

3.3.3. Qualified Ancillary International Shipping Income means net income obtained by a Constituent Entity from the following activities that are performed primarily in connection with the transportation of passengers or cargo by ships in international traffic:

(a) leasing a ship on a bare boat charter basis to another shipping enterprise that is not a Constituent Entity, provided that the charter does not exceed three years;

(b) sale of tickets issued by other shipping enterprises for the domestic leg of an international voyage;

(c) leasing and short-term storage of containers or detention charges for the late return of containers;

(d) provision of services to other shipping enterprises by engineers, maintenance staff, cargo handlers, catering staff, and customer services personnel; and

(e) investment income where the investment that generates the income is made as an integral part of the carrying on the business of operating the ships in international traffic.

3.3.4. The aggregated Qualified Ancillary International Shipping Income of all Constituent Entities located in a jurisdiction shall not exceed 50% of those Constituent Entities' International Shipping Income.

3.3.5. The costs incurred by a Constituent Entity that are directly attributable to its international shipping activities listed in Article 3.3.2 and the costs directly attributable to its qualified ancillary activities listed in Article 3.3.3 shall be deducted from the Constituent Entity's revenues from such activities to compute its International Shipping Income and Qualified Ancillary International Shipping Income. Other costs incurred by a Constituent Entity that are indirectly attributable to a Constituent Entity's international shipping activities and qualified ancillary activities shall be allocated on the basis of the Constituent Entity's revenues from such activities in proportion to its total revenues. All direct and indirect costs attributed to a Constituent Entity's International Shipping Income and Qualified Ancillary International Shipping Income shall be excluded from the computation of its GloBE Income or Loss.

3.3.6. In order for a Constituent Entity's International Shipping Income and Qualified Ancillary International Shipping Income to qualify for the exclusion from its GloBE Income or Loss under this Article, the Constituent Entity must demonstrate that the strategic or commercial management of all ships concerned is effectively carried on from within the jurisdiction where the Constituent Entity is located.

Article 3.4. Allocation of Income or Loss between a Main Entity and a Permanent Establishment

3.4.1. The Financial Accounting Net Income or Loss of a Constituent Entity that is a Permanent Establishment in accordance with paragraphs (a), (b) and (c) of the definition in Article 10.1 is the net income or loss reflected in the separate financial accounts of the Permanent Establishment. If the Permanent Establishment does not have separate financial accounts, then the Financial Accounting Net Income or Loss is the amount that would have been reflected in its separate financial accounts if prepared on a standalone basis and in accordance with the accounting standard used in the preparation of the Consolidated Financial Accounts of the Ultimate Parent Entity.

3.4.2. The Financial Accounting Net Income or Loss of a Permanent Establishment referred to in Article 3.4.1 shall be adjusted, if necessary:

(a) in the case of a Permanent Establishment as defined by paragraphs (a) and (b) of the definition in Article 10.1, to reflect only the amounts and items of income and expense that are attributable to the Permanent Establishment in accordance with the applicable Tax Treaty or domestic law of the jurisdiction where it is located regardless of the amount of income subject to tax and the amount of deductible expenses in that jurisdiction;

(b) in the case of a Permanent Establishment as defined by paragraph (c) of the definition in Article 10.1, to reflect only the amounts and items of income and expense that would have been attributed to it in accordance with Article 7 of the OECD Model Tax Convention.

3.4.3. In case of a Constituent Entity that is a Permanent Establishment in accordance with paragraph (d) of the definition in Article 10.1, its income used for computing Financial Accounting Net Income or Loss is the income being exempted in the jurisdiction where the Main Entity is located and attributable to the operations conducted outside that jurisdiction. The expenses used for computing Financial Accounting Net Income or Loss are those that are not deducted for taxable purposes in the jurisdiction where the Main Entity is located and that are attributable to such operations.

3.4.4. The Financial Accounting Net Income or Loss of a Permanent Establishment is not taken into account in determining the GloBE Income or Loss of the Main Entity, except as provided in Article 3.4.5.

3.4.5. A GloBE Loss of a Permanent Establishment shall be treated as an expense of the Main Entity (and not of the Permanent Establishment) for purposes of computing its GloBE Income or Loss to the extent that the loss of the Permanent Establishment is treated as an expense in the computation of the domestic taxable income of such Main Entity and is not set off against an item of income that is subject to tax under the laws of both the jurisdiction of the Main Entity and the jurisdiction of the Permanent Establishment. GloBE Income subsequently arising in the Permanent Establishment shall be treated as GloBE Income of the Main Entity (and not the Permanent Establishment) up to the amount of the GloBE Loss that previously was treated as an expense for purposes of computing the GloBE Income or Loss of the Main Entity.

Article 3.5. Allocation of Income or Loss from a Flow-through Entity

3.5.1. The Financial Accounting Net Income or Loss of a Constituent Entity that is a Flow-through Entity is allocated as follows:

(a) in the case of a Permanent Establishment through which the business of the Entity is wholly or partly carried out, the Financial Accounting Net Income or Loss of the Entity is allocated to that Permanent Establishment in accordance with Article 3.4;

(b) in the case of a Tax Transparent Entity that is not the Ultimate Parent Entity, any Financial Accounting Net Income or Loss remaining after application of paragraph (a) is allocated to its Constituent Entity-owners in accordance with their Ownership Interests; and

(c) in the case of a Tax Transparent Entity that is the Ultimate Parent Entity or a Reverse Hybrid Entity, any Financial Accounting Net Income or Loss remaining after application of paragraph (a) is allocated to it.

3.5.2. The rules of Article 3.5.1 shall be applied separately with respect to each Ownership Interest in the Flow-through Entity.

3.5.3. Prior to the application of Article 3.5.1, the Financial Accounting Net Income or Loss of a

Flow-through Entity shall be reduced by the amount allocable to its owners that are not Group Entities and that hold their Ownership Interest in the Flow-through Entity directly or through a Tax Transparent Structure.

3.5.4. Article 3.5.3 does not apply to:

(a) an Ultimate Parent Entity that is a Flow-through Entity; or

(b) any Flow-through Entity owned by such an Ultimate Parent Entity (directly or through a Tax Transparent Structure).

The treatment of these Entities is addressed in Article 7.1.

3.5.5. The Financial Accounting Net Income or Loss of a Flow-through Entity is reduced by the amount that is allocated to another Constituent Entity.

4 Computation of Adjusted Covered Taxes

Operation of the rules in this chapter

Under this chapter the amount of a Constituent Entity's Covered Taxes, as defined in Article 4.2 is determined

- by taking the current taxes determined for the Constituent Entity for the Fiscal Year in accordance with Article 4.1, adjusted to reflect certain timing differences under Article 4.4 and Article 4.5; by allocating Covered Taxes from one Constituent Entity to another in certain cases under Article 4.3; and
- by taking into account the effect of certain post-filing tax adjustments under Article 4.6.

Article 4.1. Adjusted Covered Taxes

4.1.1. The Adjusted Covered Taxes of a Constituent Entity for the Fiscal Year shall be equal to the current tax expense accrued in its Financial Accounting Net Income or Loss with respect to Covered Taxes for the Fiscal Year adjusted by:

(a) the net amount of its Additions to Covered Taxes for the Fiscal Year (as determined under Article 4.1.2) and Reductions to Covered Taxes for the Fiscal Year (as determined under Article 4.1.3);

(b) the Total Deferred Tax Adjustment Amount (as determined under Article 4.4); and

(c) any increase or decrease in Covered Taxes recorded in equity or Other Comprehensive Income relating to amounts included in the computation of GloBE Income or Loss that will be subject to tax under local tax rules.

4.1.2. The Additions to Covered Taxes of a Constituent Entity for the Fiscal Year is the sum of:

(a) any amount of Covered Taxes accrued as an expense in the profit before taxation in the financial accounts;

(b) any amount of GloBE Loss Deferred Tax Asset used under Article 4.5.3;

(c) any amount of Covered Taxes that is paid in the Fiscal Year and that relates to an uncertain tax position where that amount has been treated for a previous Fiscal Year as a Reduction to Covered Taxes under Article 4.1.3(d); and

(d) any amount of credit or refund in respect of a Qualified Refundable Tax Credit that is recorded as a reduction to the current tax expense.

4.1.3. The Reductions to Covered Taxes of a Constituent Entity for the Fiscal Year is the sum of:

(a) the amount of current tax expense with respect to income excluded from the computation of GloBE Income or Loss under Chapter 3;

(b) any amount of credit or refund in respect of a Non-Qualified Refundable Tax Credit that is not recorded as a reduction to the current tax expense;

(c) any amount of Covered Taxes refunded or credited, except for any Qualified Refundable Tax Credit, to a Constituent Entity that was not treated as an adjustment to current tax expense in the financial accounts;

(d) the amount of current tax expense which relates to an uncertain tax position; and

(e) any amount of current tax expense that is not expected to be paid within three years of the last day of the Fiscal Year.

4.1.4. No amount of Covered Taxes may be taken into account more than once.

4.1.5. In a Fiscal Year in which there is no Net GloBE Income for a jurisdiction, if the Adjusted Covered Taxes for a jurisdiction are less than zero and less than the Expected Adjusted Covered Taxes Amount the Constituent Entities in that jurisdiction shall be treated as having Additional Current Top-up Tax for the jurisdiction under Article 5.4 arising in the current Fiscal Year equal to the difference between these amounts. The Expected Adjusted Covered Taxes Amount is equal to the GloBE Income or Loss for a jurisdiction multiplied by the Minimum Rate.

Article 4.2. Definition of Covered Taxes

4.2.1. Covered Taxes means:

(a) Taxes recorded in the financial accounts of a Constituent Entity with respect to its income or profits or its share of the income or profits of a Constituent Entity in which it owns an Ownership Interest;

(b) Taxes on distributed profits, deemed profit distributions, and non-business expenses imposed under an Eligible Distribution Tax System;

(c) Taxes imposed in lieu of a generally applicable corporate income tax; and

(d) Taxes levied by reference to retained earnings and corporate equity, including a Tax on multiple components based on income and equity.

4.2.2. Covered Taxes does not include any amount of:

(a) Top-up Tax accrued by a Parent Entity under a Qualified IIR;

(b) Top-up Tax accrued by a Constituent Entity under a Qualified Domestic Minimum Top-Up Tax;

(c) Taxes attributable to an adjustment made by a Constituent Entity as a result of the application of a Qualified UTPR;

(d) A Disqualified Refundable Imputation Tax;

(e) Taxes paid by an insurance company in respect of returns to policyholders.

Article 4.3. Allocation of Covered Taxes from one Constituent Entity to another Constituent Entity

4.3.1. Article 4.3.2 applies to the allocation of Covered Taxes in respect of Permanent Establishments, Tax Transparent Entities and Hybrid Entities as well as the allocation of CFC taxes and taxes on distributions from one Constituent Entity to another.

4.3.2. Covered Taxes are allocated from one Constituent Entity to another Constituent Entity as follows:

(a) the amount of any Covered Taxes included in the financial accounts of a Constituent Entity with respect to GloBE Income or Loss of a Permanent Establishment is allocated to the Permanent Establishment;

(b) the amount of any Covered Taxes included in the financial accounts of a Tax Transparent Entity with respect to GloBE Income or Loss allocated to a Constituent Entity-owner pursuant to Article 3.5.1(b) is allocated to that Constituent Entity-owner;

(c) in the case of a Constituent Entity whose Constituent Entity-owners are subject to a Controlled Foreign Company Tax Regime, the amount of any Covered Taxes included in the financial accounts of its direct or indirect Constituent Entity-owners under a Controlled Foreign Company Tax Regime on their share of the Controlled Foreign Company's income are allocated to the Constituent Entity;

(d) in the case of a Constituent Entity that is a Hybrid Entity the amount of any Covered Taxes included in the financial accounts of a Constituent Entity-owner on income of the Hybrid Entity is allocated to the Hybrid Entity; and

(e) the amount of any Covered Taxes accrued in the financial accounts of a Constituent Entity's direct Constituent Entity-owners on distributions from the Constituent Entity during the Fiscal Year are allocated to the distributing Constituent Entity.

4.3.3. Covered Taxes allocated to a Constituent Entity pursuant to Article 4.3.2(c) and (d) in respect of Passive Income are included in such Constituent Entity's Adjusted Covered Taxes in an amount equal to the lesser of:

(a) the Covered Taxes allocated in respect of such Passive Income; or

(b) the Top-up Tax Percentage for the Constituent Entity's jurisdiction, determined without regard to the Covered Taxes incurred with respect to such Passive Income by the Constituent Entity-owner, multiplied by the amount of the Constituent Entity's Passive Income includible under any Controlled Foreign Company Tax Regime or fiscal transparency rule.

Any Covered Taxes of the Constituent Entity-owner incurred with respect to such Passive Income that remain after the application of this Article shall not be allocated under Article 4.3.2(c) or (d).

4.3.4. Where the GloBE Income of a Permanent Establishment is treated as GloBE Income of the Main Entity pursuant to Article 3.4.5, any Covered Taxes arising in the location of the Permanent Establishment and associated with such income are treated as Covered Taxes of the Main Entity up to an amount not exceeding such income multiplied by the highest corporate tax rate on ordinary income in the jurisdiction where the Main Entity is located.

Article 4.4. Mechanism to address temporary differences

4.4.1. The Total Deferred Tax Adjustment Amount for a Constituent Entity for the Fiscal Year is equal to the deferred tax expense accrued in its financial accounts if the applicable tax rate is below the Minimum Rate or, in any other case, such deferred tax expense recast at the Minimum Rate, with respect to Covered Taxes for the Fiscal Year subject to the adjustments set forth in Articles 4.4.2 and 4.4.3 and the following exclusions:

(a) The amount of deferred tax expense with respect to items excluded from the computation of GloBE Income or Loss under Chapter 3;

(b) The amount of deferred tax expense with respect to Disallowed Accruals and Unclaimed Accruals;

(c) The impact of a valuation adjustment or accounting recognition adjustment with respect to a deferred tax asset;

(d) The amount of deferred tax expense arising from a re-measurement with respect to a change in the applicable domestic tax rate; and

(e) The amount of deferred tax expense with respect to the generation and use of tax credits.

4.4.2. The Total Deferred Tax Adjustment Amount is adjusted as follows:

(a) Increased by the amount of any Disallowed Accrual or Unclaimed Accrual paid during the Fiscal Year;

(b) Increased by the amount of any Recaptured Deferred Tax Liability determined in a preceding Fiscal Year which has been paid during the Fiscal Year; and

(c) Reduced by the amount that would be a reduction to the Total Deferred Tax Adjustment Amount due to recognition of a loss deferred tax asset for a current year tax loss, where a loss deferred tax asset has not been recognised because the recognition criteria are not met.

4.4.3. A deferred tax asset that has been recorded at a rate lower than the Minimum Rate may be recast at the Minimum Rate in the Fiscal Year such deferred tax asset is recorded, if the taxpayer can demonstrate that the deferred tax asset is attributable to a GloBE Loss. The Total Deferred Tax Adjustment Amount is reduced by the amount that a deferred tax asset is increased due to being recast under this Article.

4.4.4. To the extent a deferred tax liability, that is not a Recapture Exception Accrual, is taken into account under this Article and such amount is not paid within the five subsequent Fiscal Years, the amount must be recaptured pursuant to this article. The Amount of the Recaptured Deferred Tax Liability determined for the current Fiscal Year shall be treated as a reduction to Covered Taxes in the fifth preceding Fiscal Year and the Effective Tax Rate and Top-up Tax of such Fiscal Year shall be recalculated under the rules of Article 5.4.1. The Recaptured Deferred Tax Liability for the current Fiscal Year is the amount of the increase in a category of deferred tax liability that was included in the Total Deferred Tax Adjustment Amount in the fifth preceding Fiscal Year that has not reversed by the end of the last day of the current Fiscal Year, unless such amount relates to a Recapture Exception Accrual as set forth in Article 4.4.5.

4.4.5. Recapture Exception Accrual means the tax expense accrued attributable to changes in associated deferred tax liabilities, in respect of:

(a) Cost recovery allowances on tangible assets

(b) The cost of a licence or similar arrangement from the government for the use of immovable property or exploitation of natural resources that entails significant investment in tangible assets;

(c) Research and development expenses;

(d) De-commissioning and remediation expenses;

(e) Fair value accounting on unrealised net gains;

(f) Foreign currency exchange net gains;

(g) Insurance reserves and insurance policy deferred acquisition costs;

(h) Gains from the sale of tangible property located in the same jurisdiction as the Constituent Entity that are reinvested in tangible property in the same jurisdiction; and

(i) Additional amounts accrued as a result of accounting principle changes with respect to categories (a) through (h).

4.4.6. Disallowed Accrual means:

(a) Any movement in deferred tax expense accrued in the financial accounts of a Constituent Entity which relates to an uncertain tax position; and

(b) Any movement in deferred tax expense accrued in the financial accounts of a Constituent Entity which relates to distributions from a Constituent Entity.

4.4.7. Unclaimed Accrual means any increase in a deferred tax liability recorded in the financial accounts of a Constituent Entity for a Fiscal Year that is not expected to be paid within the time period set forth in Article 4.4.4 and for which the Filing Constituent Entity makes an Annual Election not to include in Total Deferred Tax Adjustment Amount for such Fiscal Year.

Article 4.5. The GloBE Loss Election

4.5.1. In lieu of applying the rules set forth in Article 4.4, a Filing Constituent Entity may make a GloBE Loss Election for a jurisdiction. When a GloBE Loss Election is made for a jurisdiction, a GloBE Loss Deferred Tax Asset is established in each Fiscal Year in which there is a Net GloBE Loss for the jurisdiction. The GloBE Loss Deferred Tax Asset is equal to the Net GloBE Loss in a Fiscal Year for the jurisdiction multiplied by the Minimum Rate.

4.5.2. The balance of the GloBE Loss Deferred Tax Asset is carried forward to subsequent Fiscal Years, reduced by the amount of GloBE Loss Deferred Tax Asset used in a Fiscal Year.

4.5.3. The GloBE Loss Deferred Tax Asset must be used in any subsequent Fiscal Year in which there is Net GloBE Income for the jurisdiction in an amount equal to the lower of the Net GloBE Income multiplied by the Minimum Rate or the amount of available GloBE Loss Deferred Tax Asset.

4.5.4. If the GloBE Loss Election is subsequently revoked, any remaining GloBE Loss Deferred Tax Asset is reduced to zero, effective as of the first day of the first Fiscal Year in which the GloBE Loss Election is no longer applicable.

4.5.5. The GloBE Loss Election must be filed with the first GloBE Information Return of the MNE Group that includes the jurisdiction for which the election is made. A GloBE Loss Election cannot be made for a jurisdiction with an Eligible Distribution Tax System as defined in Article 7.3.

4.5.6. A Flow-through Entity that is a UPE of an MNE Group may make a GloBE Loss Election under this Article. When such an election is made, the GloBE Loss Deferred Tax Asset shall be calculated in accordance with Articles 4.5.1 to 4.5.5, however, the GloBE Loss Deferred Tax Asset shall be calculated with reference to the GloBE Loss of the Flow-through Entity after reduction in accordance with Article 7.1.2.

Article 4.6. Post-filing Adjustments and Tax Rate Changes

4.6.1. An adjustment to a Constituent Entity's liability for Covered Taxes for a previous Fiscal Year recorded in the financial accounts shall be treated as an adjustment to Covered Taxes in the Fiscal Year in which the adjustment is made, unless the adjustment relates to a Fiscal Year in which there is a decrease in Covered Taxes for the jurisdiction. In the case of a decrease in Covered Taxes included in the Constituent Entity's Adjusted Covered Taxes for a previous Fiscal Year, the Effective Tax Rate and Top-up Tax for such Fiscal Year must be recalculated under Article 5.4.1. In the Article 5.4.1 recalculations, the Adjusted Covered Taxes determined for the Fiscal Year shall be reduced by the amount of the decrease in Covered Taxes and GloBE Income determined for the Fiscal Year and any intervening Fiscal Years shall be adjusted as necessary and appropriate. A Filing Constituent Entity may make an Annual Election to treat an immaterial decrease in Covered Taxes as an adjustment to Covered Taxes in the Fiscal Year in which the adjustment is made. An immaterial decrease in Covered Taxes is an aggregate decrease of less than EUR 1 million in the Adjusted Covered Taxes determined for the jurisdiction for a Fiscal Year.

4.6.2. The amount of deferred tax expense resulting from a reduction to the applicable domestic tax rate shall be treated as an adjustment to a Constituent Entity's liability for Covered Taxes claimed under Article 4.1 for a previous Fiscal Year when such reduction results in the application of a rate that is less than the Minimum Rate.

4.6.3. The amount of deferred tax expense, when paid, that has resulted from an increase to the applicable domestic tax rate shall be treated as an adjustment under Article 4.6.1 to a Constituent Entity's liability for Covered Taxes claimed under Article 4.1 for a previous Fiscal Year when such amount was originally recorded at a rate less than the Minimum Rate. This adjustment is limited to an amount that is equal to an increase of deferred tax expense up to such deferred tax expense recast at the Minimum Rate.

4.6.4. If more than EUR 1 million of the amount accrued by a Constituent Entity as current tax expense and included in Adjusted Covered Taxes for a Fiscal Year is not paid within three years of the last day of such year, the Effective Tax Rate and Top-up Tax for the Fiscal Year in which the unpaid amount was claimed as a Covered Tax must be recalculated in accordance with Article 5.4.1 by excluding such unpaid amount from Adjusted Covered Taxes.

5 Computation of Effective Tax Rate and Top-up Tax

Operation of the rules in this chapter

Under this chapter the Top-up Tax of each Low-Taxed Constituent Entity is determined:

- by aggregating each Constituent Entity's GloBE Income or Loss, determined under Chapter 3, and Adjusted Covered Taxes, determined under Chapter 4, with those of other Constituent Entities located in the same jurisdiction to determine an Effective Tax Rate for the jurisdiction;
- by identifying which jurisdiction is a Low-Tax Jurisdiction (i.e. has an Effective Tax Rate that is below the Minimum Rate);
- by computing a jurisdictional Top-Up Tax Percentage for each Low-Tax Jurisdiction;
- by applying the Substance-based Income Exclusion to the Net GloBE Income in the Low-Tax Jurisdiction to determine the Excess Profits in that jurisdiction;
- by multiplying the Top-up Tax percentage by such Excess Profit and reducing the result by the amount of any Qualified Domestic Minimum Top-up Tax to determine the Top-Up Tax for each Low-Tax Jurisdiction; and
- by allocating such Top-up Taxes to the Constituent Entities in the Low-Tax Jurisdiction in proportion to their GloBE Income.

The resulting Top-up Tax of each Low Tax Constituent Entity is then charged to a Parent Entity or to Constituent Entities located in a UTPR Jurisdiction under Chapter 2.

This chapter also includes a *de minimis* exclusion for the Constituent Entities located in the same jurisdiction when their aggregated revenue and income does not exceed certain thresholds. Special rules are provided in Article 5.6 for calculating the ETR in respect of Minority-Owned Constituent Entities.

Article 5.1. Determination of Effective Tax Rate

5.1.1. The Effective Tax Rate of the MNE Group for a jurisdiction with Net GloBE Income shall be calculated for each Fiscal Year. The Effective Tax Rate of the MNE Group for a jurisdiction is equal to the sum of the Adjusted Covered Taxes of each Constituent Entity located in the jurisdiction divided by the Net GloBE Income of the jurisdiction for the Fiscal Year. For purposes of Chapter 5, each Stateless Constituent Entity shall be treated as a single Constituent Entity located in a separate jurisdiction.

5.1.2. The Net GloBE Income of a jurisdiction for a Fiscal Year is the positive amount, if any, computed in accordance with the following formula:

$$Net\ GloBE\ Income = GloBE\ Income\ of\ all\ Constituent\ Entities - GloBE\ Losses\ of\ all\ Constituent\ Entities$$

Where:

(a) the GloBE Income of all Constituent Entities is the sum of the GloBE Income of all Constituent Entities located in the jurisdiction determined in accordance with Chapter 3 for the Fiscal Year; and

(b) the GloBE Losses of all Constituent Entities is the sum of the GloBE Losses of all Constituent Entities located in the jurisdiction determined in accordance with Chapter 3 for the Fiscal Year.

5.1.3. Adjusted Covered Taxes and GloBE Income or Loss of Constituent Entities that are Investment Entities are excluded from the determination of the Effective Tax Rate in Article 5.1.1 and the determination of Net GloBE Income in Article 5.1.2.

Article 5.2. Top-up Tax

5.2.1. The Top-up Tax Percentage for a jurisdiction for a Fiscal Year shall be the positive percentage point difference, if any, computed in accordance with the following formula:

$$Top\ up\ Tax\ Percentage = Minimum\ Rate - Effective\ Tax\ Rate$$

Where the Effective Tax Rate is the Effective Tax Rate determined in accordance with Article 5.1 for the jurisdiction for the Fiscal Year.

5.2.2. The Excess Profit for the jurisdiction for the Fiscal Year is the positive amount, if any, computed in accordance with the following formula:

$$Excess\ Profit = Net\ GloBE\ Income - Substance\ based\ Income\ Exclusion$$

Where:

(a) The Net GloBE Income is the Net GloBE Income determined under Article 5.1.2 for the jurisdiction for the Fiscal Year; and

(b) The Substance-based Income Exclusion is the Substance-based Income Exclusion determined under Article 5.3 for the jurisdiction for the Fiscal Year (if any).

5.2.3. The Jurisdictional Top-up Tax for a jurisdiction for a Fiscal Year is equal to the positive amount, if any, computed in accordance with the following formula:

$$Jurisdictional\ Top\ up\ Tax = (Top\ up\ Tax\ Percentage\ x\ Excess\ Profit) + Additional\ Current\ Top\ up\ Tax - Domestic\ Top\ up\ Tax$$

Where:

(a) The Top-up Tax Percentage is percentage point difference determined in accordance with Article 5.2.1 for the jurisdiction for the Fiscal Year;

(b) The Excess Profit is the Excess Profit determined in accordance with Article 5.2.2 for the jurisdiction for the Fiscal Year;

(c) The Additional Current Top-up Tax is the amount determined, or treated as Additional Current Top-up Tax, under Article 4.1.5 or Article 5.4.1 for the jurisdiction for the Fiscal Year; and

(d) The Domestic Top-up Tax is the amount payable under a Qualified Domestic Minimum Top-Up Tax of the jurisdiction for the Fiscal Year.

5.2.4. Except as provided in Article 5.4.3, the Top-up Tax of a Constituent Entity shall be determined for each Constituent Entity of a jurisdiction that has GloBE Income determined in accordance with Chapter 3 for the Fiscal Year included in the computation of Net GloBE Income of that jurisdiction in accordance with the following formula:

$$Top\ up\ Tax\ of\ a\ CE = Jurisdictional\ Top\ up\ Tax \times \frac{GloBE\ Income\ of\ the\ CE}{Aggregate\ GloBE\ Income\ of\ all\ CEs}$$

Where:

(a) The Jurisdictional Top-up Tax is the Top-up Tax determined in accordance with Article 5.2.3 for the jurisdiction for the Fiscal Year;

(b) The GloBE Income of the CE is the GloBE Income of the Constituent Entity determined in accordance with Article 3.2 for the jurisdiction for the Fiscal Year;

(c) The aggregate GloBE Income of all CEs is the aggregate GloBE Income of all Constituent Entities that have GloBE Income for the Fiscal Year included in the computation of Net GloBE Income in accordance with Article 5.1.2 for the jurisdiction for the Fiscal Year.

5.2.5. If the Jurisdictional Top-up Tax is attributable to a recalculation under the Article 5.4.1 and the jurisdiction does not have Net GloBE Income for the current Fiscal Year, Top-up Tax shall be allocated using the formula in Article 5.2.4 based on the GloBE Income of the Constituent Entities in the Fiscal Years for which the recalculations under Article 5.4.1 were performed.

Article 5.3. Substance-based Income Exclusion

5.3.1. The Net GloBE Income for the jurisdiction shall be reduced by the Substance-based Income Exclusion for the jurisdiction to determine the Excess Profit for purposes of computing the Top-up Tax under Article 5.2. A Filing Constituent Entity of an MNE Group may make an Annual Election not to apply the Substance-based Income Exclusion for a jurisdiction by not computing the exclusion or claiming it in the computation of Top-up Tax for the jurisdiction in the GloBE Information Return(s) filed for the Fiscal Year.

5.3.2. The Substance-based Income Exclusion amount for a jurisdiction is the sum of the payroll carve-out and the tangible asset carve-out for each Constituent Entity, except for Constituent Entities that are Investment Entities, in that jurisdiction.

5.3.3. The payroll carve-out for a Constituent Entity located in a jurisdiction is equal to 5% of its Eligible Payroll Costs of Eligible Employees that perform activities for the MNE Group in such jurisdiction, except Eligible Payroll costs that are:

(a) capitalised and included in the carrying value of Eligible Tangible Assets;

(b) attributable to a Constituent Entity's International Shipping Income and Qualified Ancillary International Shipping Income under Article 3.3.5 that is excluded from the computation of GloBE Income or Loss for the Fiscal Year.

5.3.4. The tangible asset carve-out for a Constituent Entity located in a jurisdiction is equal to 5% of the carrying value of Eligible Tangible Assets located in such jurisdiction. Eligible Tangible Assets means:

(a) property, plant, and equipment located in that jurisdiction;

(b) natural resources located in that jurisdiction;

(c) a lessee's right of use of tangible assets located in that jurisdiction; and

(d) a licence or similar arrangement from the government for the use of immovable property or exploitation of natural resources that entails significant investment in tangible assets.

For this purpose, the tangible asset carve-out computation shall not include the carrying value of property (including land or buildings) that is held for sale, lease or investment. The tangible asset carve-out computation shall not include the carrying value of tangible assets used in the generation of a Constituent Entity's International Shipping Income and Qualified Ancillary International Shipping Income (i.e. ships and other maritime equipment and infrastructure). The carrying value of tangible assets attributable to a Constituent Entity's excess income over the cap for Qualified Ancillary International Shipping Income under Article 3.3.4 shall be included in the tangible asset carve-out computation.

5.3.5. The computation of carrying value of Eligible Tangible Assets for purposes of Article 5.3.4 shall be based on the average of the carrying value (net of accumulated depreciation, amortisation, or depletion and including any amount attributable to capitalisation of payroll expense) at the beginning and ending of the Reporting Fiscal Year as recorded for the purposes of preparing the Consolidated Financial Statements of the Ultimate Parent Entity.

5.3.6. For purposes of Articles 5.3.3 and 5.3.4, the Eligible Payroll Costs and Eligible Tangible Assets of a Constituent Entity that is a Permanent Establishment are those included in its separate financial accounts as determined by Article 3.4.1 and adjusted in accordance with Article 3.4.2, provided that the Eligible Employees and Eligible Tangible Assets are located in the jurisdiction where the Permanent Establishment is located. The Eligible Payroll Costs and Eligible Tangible Assets of a Permanent Establishment are not taken into account for the Eligible Payroll Costs and Eligible Tangible Assets of the Main Entity. The Eligible Payroll Costs and Eligible Tangible Assets of a Permanent Establishment whose income has been wholly or partly excluded in accordance with Articles 3.5.3 and 7.1.4 are excluded from the Substance-based Income Exclusion computations of the MNE Group in the same proportion.

5.3.7. For purposes of Articles 5.3.3 and 5.3.4, Eligible Payroll Costs and Eligible Tangible Assets of a Flow-through Entity that are not allocated under Article 5.3.6 are allocated as follows:

(a) if the Financial Accounting Net Income or Loss of the Flow-through Entity has been allocated to the Constituent Entity-owner under Article 3.5.1(b), then the Entity's Eligible Payroll Costs and Eligible Tangible Assets are allocated in the same proportion to the Constituent Entity-owner provided it is located in the jurisdiction where the Eligible Employees and Eligible Tangible Assets are located;

(b) if the Flow-through Entity is the Ultimate Parent Entity, then Eligible Payroll Costs and Eligible Tangible Assets located in the jurisdiction where the Ultimate Parent Entity is located are allocated to it and reduced in proportion to the income that is excluded under Article 7.1.1; and

(c) all other Eligible Payroll Costs and Eligible Tangible Assets of the Flow-through Entity are excluded from the Substance-based Income Exclusion computations of the MNE Group.

Article 5.4. Additional Current Top-up Tax

5.4.1. If the Effective Tax Rate and Top-up Tax for a prior Fiscal Year is required or permitted to be recalculated pursuant to an ETR Adjustment Article,

(a) the Effective Tax Rate and Top-Up Tax for the prior Fiscal Year shall be recalculated in accordance with the rules of Article 5.1 through Article 5.3 after taking into account the adjustments to Adjusted Covered Taxes and GloBE Income or Loss required by the relevant ETR Adjustment Article; and

(b) any amount of incremental Top-up Tax resulting from such recalculation shall be treated as Additional Current Top-up Tax under Article 5.2.3 arising in the current Fiscal Year.

5.4.2. If there is Additional Current Top-up Tax attributable to a recalculation under Article 5.4.1 and the jurisdiction does not have Net GloBE Income for the current Fiscal Year, the GloBE Income of each Constituent Entity located in the jurisdiction for purposes of Article 2.2.2 shall be equal to the result of the Top-up Tax allocated to such Entity under Articles 5.2.4 and 5.2.5 divided by the Minimum Rate.

5.4.3. If there is Additional Current Top-up Tax attributable to the operation of Article 4.1.5, the GloBE Income of each Constituent Entity located in the jurisdiction for purposes of Article 2.2.2 shall be equal to the result of the Top-up Tax allocated to such Entity under this Article divided by the Minimum Rate. The amount of Additional Current Top-up Tax allocated to each Constituent Entity for purposes of this Article shall be allocated only to Constituent Entities that record an Adjusted Covered Taxes amount that is less than zero and less than the GloBE Income or Loss of such Constituent Entity multiplied by the Minimum Rate. The allocation shall be made pro-rata based upon the following amount for each of those Constituent Entities:

$$(GloBE\ Income\ or\ Loss\ x\ Minimum\ Rate) - Adjusted\ Covered\ Taxes$$

5.4.4. If a Constituent Entity is allocated Additional Current top-up Tax pursuant to this Article and Article 5.2.4 such Constituent Entity shall be treated as a Low-Taxed Constituent Entity for the purposes of Chapter 2.

Article 5.5. De minimis exclusion

5.5.1. At the election of the Filing Constituent Entity, and notwithstanding the requirements otherwise provided in Chapter 5, the Top-up Tax for the Constituent Entities located in a jurisdiction shall be deemed to be zero for a Fiscal Year if, for such Fiscal Year:

(a) the Average GloBE Revenue of such jurisdiction is less than EUR 10 million; and

(b) the Average GloBE Income or Loss of such jurisdiction is a loss or is less than EUR 1 million.

The election under this Article is an Annual Election.

5.5.2. For purposes of Article 5.5.1, the Average GloBE Revenue (or GloBE Income or Loss) of a jurisdiction is the average of the GloBE Revenue (or GloBE Income or Loss) of the jurisdiction for the current and the two preceding Fiscal Years. If there were no Constituent Entities with GloBE Revenue or GloBE Losses that were located in the jurisdiction in the first or second preceding Fiscal Year, such year or years shall be excluded from the calculation of the Average GloBE Revenue and the Average GloBE Income or Loss of the relevant jurisdiction.

5.5.3. For purposes of Article 5.5.2:

(a) the GloBE Revenue of a jurisdiction for a Fiscal Year is the sum of the revenue of all Constituent Entities located in the jurisdiction for such Fiscal Year, taking into account the adjustments calculated in accordance with Chapter 3; and

(b) the GloBE Income or Loss of a jurisdiction for a Fiscal Year is the Net GloBE Income of that jurisdiction, if any, or the Net GloBE Loss of that jurisdiction.

5.5.4. An election under Article 5.5 shall not apply to a Constituent Entity that is a Stateless

Constituent Entity or an Investment Entity and the revenue and GloBE Income or Loss of a Stateless Constituent Entity and of an Investment Entity shall be excluded from the computations in Article 5.5.3.

Article 5.6. Minority-Owned Constituent Entities

5.6.1. The computation of the Effective Tax Rate and Top-up Tax for a jurisdiction in accordance with Chapters 3 to 7, and Article 8.2 with respect to members of a Minority-Owned Subgroup shall apply as if they were a separate MNE Group. The Adjusted Covered Taxes and GloBE Income or Loss of members of a Minority-Owned Subgroup are excluded from the determination of the remainder of the MNE Group's Effective Tax Rate in Article 5.1.1 and Net GloBE Income in Article 5.1.2.

5.6.2. The Effective Tax Rate and Top-up Tax of a Minority-Owned Constituent Entity that is not a member of a Minority-Owned Subgroup is computed on an entity basis in accordance with Chapters 3 to 7, and Article 8.2. The Adjusted Covered Taxes and GloBE Income or Loss of the Minority-Owned Constituent Entity are excluded from the determination of the remainder of the MNE Group's Effective Tax Rate in Article 5.1.1 and Net GloBE Income in Article 5.1.2. This provision does not apply if the Minority-Owned Constituent Entity is an Investment Entity.

6 Corporate Restructurings and Holding Structures

Operation of the rules in this chapter

Chapter 6 contains rules relating to acquisitions, disposals and Joint Ventures.

- Article 6.1 supplements Article 1.1 by providing further rules for applying the consolidated revenue threshold in the case of merger and demerger transactions that took place in the prior four year period.
- Article 6.2 provides special rules for the application of the GloBE Rules that apply when a Constituent Entity enters or leaves an MNE Group during the Fiscal Year.
- Article 6.3 provides special rules for the treatment of transfers of assets and liabilities including as part of a reorganisation.
- Article 6.4 brings certain Joint Ventures within the scope of the GloBE Rules.
- Article 6.5 provides special rules for Multi-Parented MNE Groups.

Article 6.1. Application of Consolidated Revenue Threshold to Group Mergers and Demergers

6.1.1. For the purposes of Article 1.1

(a) If two or more Groups merge to form a single Group in any of the four Fiscal Years prior to the tested Fiscal Year, then the consolidated revenue threshold of the MNE Group for any Fiscal Year prior to the merger is deemed to be met for that year if the sum of the revenue included in each of their Consolidated Financial Statements for that year is equal to or greater than EUR 750 million.

(b) Where an Entity that is not a member of any Group (target) merges with an Entity or Group (acquirer) in the tested Fiscal Year and the target or acquirer does not have Consolidated Financial Statements in any of the four Fiscal Years prior to the tested Fiscal Year because it was not a member of any Group in that year, the consolidated revenue threshold of the MNE Group is deemed to be met for that year if the sum of the revenue included in each of their Financial Statements or Consolidated Financial Statements for that year is equal to or greater than EUR 750 million.

(c) Where a single MNE Group within the scope of the GloBE Rules demerges into two or more Groups (each a demerged Group), the consolidated revenue threshold is deemed to be met by a demerged Group:

i. with respect to the first tested Fiscal Year ending after the demerger, if the demerged

Group has annual revenues of EUR 750 million or more in that year;

ii. with respect to the second to fourth tested Fiscal Years ending after the demerger, if the demerged Group has annual revenues of EUR 750 million or more in at least two of the Fiscal Years following the year of the demerger.

6.1.2. For the purposes of Article 6.1.1 a merger is any arrangement where :

(a) all or substantially all of the Group Entities of two or more separate Groups are brought under common control such that they constitute Group Entities of a combined Group; or

(b) an Entity that is not a member of any Group is brought under common control with another Entity or Group such that they constitute Group Entities of a combined Group.

6.1.3. For the purposes of Article 6.1.1 a demerger is any arrangement where the Group Entities of a single Group are separated into two or more Groups that are no longer consolidated by the same Ultimate Parent Entity.

Article 6.2. Constituent Entities joining and leaving an MNE Group

6.2.1. Except to the extent provided in Article 6.2.2, the following provisions apply where an Entity (the target) becomes or ceases to be a Constituent Entity of an MNE Group as a result of a transfer of direct or indirect Ownership Interests in such Entity during the Fiscal Year (the acquisition year):

(a) where the target joins or leaves a Group or the target becomes the Ultimate Parent Entity of a new Group, the target will be treated as a member of the Group for the purposes of the GloBE Rules if any portion of its assets, liabilities, income, expenses or cash flows are included on a line-by-line basis in the Consolidated Financial Statements of the Ultimate Parent Entity in the acquisition year;

(b) in the acquisition year, an MNE Group shall take into account only the Financial Accounting Net Income or Loss and Adjusted Covered Taxes of the target that are taken into account in the Consolidated Financial Statements of the Ultimate Parent Entity for purposes of applying the GloBE Rules;

(c) in the acquisition year and each succeeding year, the target shall determine its GloBE Income or Loss and Adjusted Covered Taxes using its historical carrying value of the assets and liabilities;

(d) the computation of the target's Eligible Payroll Costs under Article 5.3.3 shall take into account only those costs reflected in the Consolidated Financial Statements of the Ultimate Parent Entity;

(e) the computation of carrying value of the target's Eligible Tangible Assets for purposes of Article 5.3.4 shall be adjusted proportionally to correspond with the length of the relevant Fiscal Year that the target was a member of the MNE Group;

(f) with the exception of the GloBE Loss Deferred Tax Asset, the deferred tax assets and deferred tax liabilities of a Constituent Entity that are transferred between MNE Groups shall be taken into account under the GloBE Rules by the acquiring MNE Group in the same manner and to the same extent as if the acquiring MNE Group controlled the Constituent Entity when such assets and liabilities arose;

(g) deferred tax liabilities of a target that have previously been included in its Total Deferred Tax Adjustment Amount shall be treated as reversed for purposes of applying Article 4.4.4

by the disposing MNE Group and treated as arising in the acquisition year for purposes of applying Article 4.4.4 by the acquiring MNE Group, except that in such cases any subsequent reduction to Covered Taxes under Article 4.4.4 shall have effect in the year in which the amount is recaptured ; and

(h) if the target is a Parent Entity and it is a Group Entity of two or more MNE Groups during the acquisition year, it shall apply separately the provisions of the IIR to its Allocable Shares of the Top-up Tax of Low-Taxed Constituent Entities determined for each MNE Group.

6.2.2. For purposes of the GloBE Rules, the acquisition or disposal of a Controlling Interest in a Constituent Entity will be treated as an acquisition or disposal of the assets and liabilities if the jurisdiction in which the target Constituent Entity is located, or in the case of a Tax Transparent Entity, the jurisdiction in which the assets are located, treats the acquisition or disposal of that Controlling Interest in the same or similar manner as an acquisition or disposition of the assets and liabilities and imposes a Covered Tax on the seller based on the difference between the tax basis and the consideration paid in exchange for the Controlling Interest or the fair value of the assets and liabilities.

Article 6.3. Transfer of Assets and Liabilities

6.3.1. In the case of a disposition or acquisition of assets and liabilities, a disposing Constituent Entity will include the gain or loss on disposition in the computation of its GloBE Income or Loss and an acquiring Constituent Entity will determine its GloBE Income or Loss using the acquiring Constituent Entity's carrying value of the acquired assets and liabilities determined under the accounting standard used in preparing Consolidated Financial Statements of the Ultimate Parent Entity.

6.3.2. If the disposition or acquisition of assets and liabilities is part of a GloBE Reorganisation Article 6.3.1 shall not apply and:

(a) a disposing Constituent Entity will exclude any gain or loss on the disposition from the computation of its GloBE Income or Loss; and

(b) an acquiring Constituent Entity will determine its GloBE Income or Loss after the acquisition using the disposing Entity's carrying values of the acquired assets and liabilities upon disposition.

6.3.3. If a disposition or acquisition of assets and liabilities is part of a GloBE Reorganisation in which a disposing Constituent Entity recognises Non-qualifying Gain or Loss, Articles 6.3.1 and 6.3.2 shall not apply and:

(a) the disposing Constituent Entity will include gain or loss on the disposition in its GloBE Income or Loss computation to the extent of the Non-qualifying Gain or Loss; and

(b) an acquiring Constituent Entity will determine its GloBE Income or Loss after the acquisition using the disposing Entity's carrying value of the acquired assets and liabilities upon disposition adjusted consistent with local tax rules to account for the Non-qualifying Gain or Loss.

6.3.4. At the election of the Filing Constituent Entity, a Constituent Entity of an MNE Group that is required or permitted to adjust the basis of its assets and the amount of its liabilities to fair value for tax purposes in the jurisdiction in which it is located, shall:

(a) Include in the computation of its GloBE Income or Loss an amount of gain or loss in respect of each of its assets and liabilities that is equal to:

i. the difference between the carrying value for financial accounting purposes of the asset or liability immediately before and the fair value of the asset or liability immediately after the date of the event that triggered the tax adjustment (the triggering event);

ii. decreased (or increased) by the Non-Qualifying Gain (or Loss), if any, arising in connection with the triggering event;

(b) use the fair value for financial accounting purposes of the asset or liability immediately after the triggering event to determine GloBE Income or Loss in Fiscal Years ending after the triggering event; and

(c) include the net total of the amounts determined in 6.3.4(a) in the Constituent Entity's GloBE Income or Loss in one of the following ways:

i. the net total of the amounts is included in the Fiscal Year in which the triggering event occurs; or

ii. an amount equal to the net total of the amounts divided by five is included in the Fiscal Year in which the triggering event occurs and in each of the immediate four subsequent Fiscal Years, unless the Constituent Entity leaves the MNE Group in a Fiscal Year within this period, in which case the remaining amount will be wholly included in that Fiscal Year.

Article 6.4. Joint Ventures

6.4.1. The GloBE Rules shall apply to a Joint Venture and its JV Subsidiaries as follows for each Fiscal Year:

(a) Chapters 3 to 7, and Article 8.2 shall apply for purposes of computing any Top-Up Tax of the Joint Venture and its JV Subsidiaries as if they were Constituent Entities of a separate MNE Group and as if the Joint Venture was the Ultimate Parent Entity of that Group;

(b) a Parent Entity that holds directly or indirectly Ownership Interests in the Joint Venture or a JV Subsidiary shall apply the IIR with respect to its Allocable Share of the Top-up Tax of a member of the JV Group in accordance with Article 2.1 to Article 2.3; and

(c) the JV Group Top-up Tax shall be reduced by each Parent Entity's Allocable Share of the Top-up Tax of each member of the JV Group that is brought into charge under a Qualified IIR under paragraph (b), and any remaining amount shall be added to the Total UTPR Top-up Tax Amount taken into account under Article 2.5.1.

Article 6.5. Multi-Parented MNE Groups

6.5.1. The following provisions apply to Multi-Parented MNE Groups:

(a) the Entities and Constituent Entities of each Group are treated as members of a single MNE Group for purposes of the GloBE Rules (the Multi-Parented MNE Group);

(b) an Entity (other than an Excluded Entity) shall be treated as a Constituent Entity if it is consolidated on a line-by-line basis by the Multi-Parented MNE Group or its Controlling Interests are held by Entities in the Multi-Parented MNE Group;

(c) the Consolidated Financial Statements of the Multi-Parented MNE Group shall be the Consolidated Financial Statements referred to in the definition of Stapled Structure or Dual-listed arrangement (as relevant) prepared under an Acceptable Financial Accounting Standard, which is deemed to be the accounting standard of the Ultimate Parent Entity;

(d) the Ultimate Parent Entities of the separate Groups that comprise the Multi-Parented MNE Group shall be the Ultimate Parent Entities of the Multi-Parented MNE Group (when applying the GloBE Rules in respect of a Multi-Parented MNE Group, references to an Ultimate Parent Entity shall apply, as required, as if they were references to multiple Ultimate Parent Entities);

(e) the Parent Entities of the Multi-Parented MNE Group (including each Ultimate Parent Entity) located in [insert name of implementing jurisdiction] shall apply the IIR in accordance with Article 2.1 to Article 2.3 with respect to their Allocable Share of the Top-up Tax of the Low-Taxed Constituent Entity;

(f) all of the Constituent Entities of the Multi-Parented MNE Group located in [insert name of implementing jurisdiction] shall apply the UTPR in accordance with Article 2.4 to Article 2.6 taking into account the Top-up Tax of each Low-Taxed Constituent Entity of the Multi-Parented MNE Group; and

(g) the Ultimate Parent Entities are required to submit the GloBE Information Return in accordance with Article 8.1, unless they appoint a single Designated Filing Entity and that return shall include the information concerning each of the Groups that comprise the Multi-Parented MNE Group.

7 Tax neutrality and distribution regimes

Operation of the rules in this chapter

Chapter 7 deals with the application of the GloBE Rules to certain tax neutrality and other distribution regimes.

- Article 7.1 and Article 7.2 provide special rules in relation to Ultimate Parent Entities that are subject to a tax neutrality regime (such as a tax transparency regime or a Deductible Dividend Regime).
- Article 7.3 provides special rules in relation to certain tax regimes that subject an Entity to tax on its earnings when those earnings are distributed or deemed distributed.
- Article 7.4 to Article 7.6 provide special rules in relation to controlled Investment Entities that seek to preserve the tax neutrality of these Entities without giving rise to any leakage under the GloBE Rules.

Article 7.1. Ultimate Parent Entity that is a Flow-through Entity

7.1.1. The GloBE Income for a Fiscal Year of a Flow-through Entity that is the Ultimate Parent Entity of an MNE Group shall be reduced by the amount of GloBE Income attributable to each Ownership Interest if:

(a) the holder of the Ownership Interest is subject to tax on such income for a taxable period that ends within 12 months of the end of the MNE Group's Fiscal Year and:

(i) the holder of the Ownership Interest is subject to tax on the full amount of such income at a nominal rate that equals or exceeds the Minimum Rate; or

(ii) it can be reasonably expected that the aggregate amount of Adjusted Covered Taxes of the Ultimate Parent Entity and Taxes of the holder of the Ownership Interest on such income equals or exceeds the amount that results from multiplying the full amount of such income by the Minimum Rate; or

(b) the holder is a natural person that:

(i) is a tax resident in the UPE Jurisdiction; and

(ii) holds Ownership Interests that, in the aggregate, are a right to 5% or less of the profits and assets of the Ultimate Parent Entity; or

(c) the holder is a Governmental Entity, an International Organisation, a Non-profit Organisation, or a Pension Fund that

(i) is resident in the UPE Jurisdiction; and

(ii) holds Ownership Interests that, in the aggregate, are a right to 5% or less of the profits and assets of the Ultimate Parent Entity.

7.1.2. In computing its GloBE Loss for a Fiscal Year, a Flow-through Entity that is the Ultimate Parent Entity of an MNE Group shall reduce its GloBE Loss for such Fiscal Year by the amount of GloBE Loss attributable to each Ownership Interest, except to the extent that the holders of Ownership Interests are not allowed to use the loss in computing their separate taxable income.

7.1.3. A Flow-through Entity that reduces its GloBE Income pursuant to Article 7.1.1 shall reduce its Covered Taxes proportionally.

7.1.4. Articles 7.1.1 through 7.1.3 shall apply to a Permanent Establishment:

(a) through which a Flow-Through Entity that is the Ultimate Parent Entity of an MNE Group wholly or partly carries out its business; or

(b) through which the business of a Tax Transparent Entity is wholly or partly carried out if the Ultimate Parent Entity's Ownership Interest in that Tax Transparent Entity is held directly or through a Tax Transparent Structure.

Article 7.2. Ultimate Parent Entity subject to Deductible Dividend Regime

7.2.1. For purposes of computing its GloBE Income or Loss for a Fiscal year, an Ultimate Parent Entity that is subject to a Deductible Dividend Regime shall reduce (but not below zero) its GloBE Income for such Fiscal Year by the amount that is distributed as a Deductible Dividend within 12 months of the end of the Fiscal Year if:

(a) the dividend is subject to tax in the hands of the dividend recipient for a taxable period that ends within 12 months of the end of the MNE Group's Fiscal Year, and:

(i) the dividend recipient is subject to tax on such dividend at a nominal rate that equals or exceeds the Minimum Rate;

(ii) it can be reasonably expected that the aggregate amount of Adjusted Covered Taxes of the Ultimate Parent Entity and Taxes paid by the dividend recipient on the dividend income equals or exceeds the amount that results from multiplying the full amount of such income by the Minimum Rate; or

(iii) the dividend recipient is a natural person and the dividend is a patronage dividend from a supply Cooperative; or

(b) the dividend recipient is a natural person that:

(i) is a tax resident in the UPE Jurisdiction; and

(ii) holds Ownership Interests that, in the aggregate, are a right to 5% or less of the profits and assets of the Ultimate Parent Entity.

(c) the dividend recipient is resident in the UPE Jurisdiction and is:

(i) a Governmental Entity,

(ii) an International Organisation,

(iii) a Non-profit Organisation or

(iv) a Pension Fund that is not a Pension Services Entity.

7.2.2. An Ultimate Parent Entity that reduces its GloBE Income pursuant to Article 7.2.1 shall reduce its Covered Taxes (other than the Taxes for which the dividend deduction was allowed) proportionally and shall reduce its GloBE Income by the same amount.

7.2.3. If the Ultimate Parent Entity holds an Ownership Interest in another Constituent Entity subject to the Deductible Dividend Regime (directly or through a chain of such Constituent Entities), Articles 7.2.1 and 7.2.2 shall apply to each other Constituent Entity in the UPE Jurisdiction that is subject to the Deductible Dividend Regime to the extent that its GloBE Income is further distributed by the Ultimate Parent Entity to recipients that meet the requirements of Article 7.2.1.

7.2.4. Patronage dividends from a supply Cooperative are subject to tax to the extent they reduce an expense or cost that is deductible in the computation of the recipient's taxable income.

Article 7.3. Eligible Distribution Tax Systems

7.3.1. A Filing Constituent Entity may make an annual election with respect to a Constituent Entity that is subject to an Eligible Distribution Tax System to add the amount of Deemed Distribution Tax determined under Article 7.3.2 to Adjusted Covered Taxes for the Fiscal Year. An election under this Article shall apply to all Constituent Entities located in the jurisdiction.

7.3.2. The amount of Deemed Distribution Tax is the lesser of:

(a) the amount of Adjusted Covered Taxes necessary to increase the Effective Tax Rate computed under Article 5.2.1 for the jurisdiction for the Fiscal Year to the Minimum Rate; or

(b) the amount of tax that would have been due if the Constituent Entities located in the jurisdiction had distributed all of their income that is subject to the Eligible Distribution Tax Regime during such year.

7.3.3. An annual Deemed Distribution Tax Recapture Account is established for each Fiscal Year in which the election in Article 7.3.1 applies. A Deemed Distribution Tax Recapture Account is increased by the amount of the Deemed Distribution Tax determined under Article 7.3.2 for the jurisdiction for the Fiscal Year for which it was established. At the end of each succeeding Fiscal Year, the outstanding balances of Deemed Distribution Tax Recapture Accounts established for prior Fiscal Years are reduced in chronological order and to the extent thereof, but not below zero:

(a) first by Taxes paid by the Constituent Entities during the Fiscal Year in relation to actual or deemed distributions;

(b) then by the amount of any Net GloBE Loss of the jurisdiction multiplied by the Minimum Rate; and

(c) then by any amount of Recapture Account Loss Carry-forward applied to the current Fiscal Year pursuant to Article 7.3.4.

7.3.4. A Recapture Account Loss Carry-forward shall be established for the jurisdiction when the amount described in Article 7.3.3(b) exceeds the outstanding balance of the Deemed Distribution Tax Recapture Accounts. The Recapture Account Loss Carry-forward shall be in an amount equal to such excess and shall be taken into account in subsequent Fiscal Years as a reduction to Deemed Distribution Tax Recapture Accounts in such Fiscal Years. When such amount is taken into account in a subsequent Fiscal Year, the Recapture Account Loss Carry-forward must be reduced by that amount.

7.3.5. If there is an outstanding balance of a Deemed Distribution Tax Recapture Account (maintained in accordance with Article 7.3.3) on the last day of the fourth Fiscal Year after the Fiscal

Year for which such account was established, the Effective Tax Rate and Top-up Tax for the Fiscal Year for which the account was established must be recalculated under Article 5.4.1 by treating the balance of the Deemed Distribution Tax Recapture Account as a reduction to the Adjusted Covered Taxes previously determined for such year.

7.3.6. Taxes paid during the Fiscal Year in relation to actual or deemed distributions are not included in Adjusted Covered Taxes to the extent they reduce a Deemed Distribution Tax Recapture Account under Article 7.3.3.

7.3.7. In the Fiscal Year that a Departing Constituent Entity leaves the MNE Group or transfers substantially all of its assets,

(a) the Effective Tax Rate and Top-up Tax for each preceding year for which a Deemed Distribution Tax Recapture Account is outstanding is re-calculated in accordance with the principles of Article 5.4.1. by treating the balance of the Deemed Distribution Tax Recapture Account as a reduction to the Adjusted Covered Taxes previously determined for such year; and

(b) any amount of incremental Top-up Tax resulting from such recalculation shall be multiplied by the Disposition Recapture Ratio to determine the Additional Current Top-up Tax for purposes of Article 5.2.3.

7.3.8. The Disposition Recapture Ratio is determined for each Departing Constituent Entity using the following formula:

$$\frac{GloBE\ Income\ of\ the\ CE}{Net\ Income\ of\ the\ jurisdiction}$$

Where:

(a) GloBE Income of the CE is the sum of GloBE Income of the Departing Constituent Entity determined in accordance with Chapter 3 for each Fiscal Year corresponding to the Deemed Distribution Tax Recapture Accounts for the jurisdiction; and

(b) Net Income of the jurisdiction is the sum of the Net GloBE Income of the jurisdiction determined In accordance with Article 5.1.2 for each Fiscal Year corresponding to the Deemed Distribution Tax Recapture Accounts for the jurisdiction.

Article 7.4. Effective Tax Rate Computation for Investment Entities

7.4.1. The rules of Article 7.4 apply to Constituent Entities that meet the definition of an Investment Entity, except Investment Entities that are Tax Transparent Entities or subject to an election under Article 7.5 or Article 7.6.

7.4.2. The Effective Tax Rate for an Investment Entity that is a Constituent Entity shall be calculated separately from the Effective Tax Rate of the jurisdiction in which it is located. The Effective Tax Rate for each such Investment Entity is equal to the Investment Entity's Adjusted Covered Taxes divided by the MNE Group's Allocable Share of the Investment Entity's GloBE Income determined under Chapter 3. If there is more than one Investment Entity located in the jurisdiction, the Adjusted Covered Taxes and the MNE Group's Allocable Share of each Investment Entity's GloBE Income or Loss determined for each such Investment Entity are combined to compute the Effective Tax Rate of all such Investment Entities.

7.4.3. An Investment Entity's Adjusted Covered Taxes is the sum of the Adjusted Covered Taxes determined for the Investment Entity under Article 4.1 attributable to the MNE Group's Allocable Share of the Investment Entity's GloBE Income and the Covered Taxes allocated to the Investment

Entity under Article 4.3. The Investment Entity's Adjusted Covered Taxes does not include any Covered Taxes accrued by the Investment Entity attributable to income that is not part of the MNE Group's Allocable Share of the Investment Entity's GloBE Income.

7.4.4. The MNE Group's Allocable Share of the Investment Entity's GloBE Income is equal to the Allocable Share of the Investment Entity's GloBE Income or Loss that would be determined for the Ultimate Parent Entity in accordance with the rules of Article 2.2.2 taking into account only interests that are not subject to an election under Article 7.5 or Article 7.6.

7.4.5. The Top-up Tax of a Constituent Entity that is an Investment Entity shall be an amount equal to the Top-up Tax Percentage for the Investment Entity multiplied by the excess of the MNE Group's Allocable Share of the Investment Entity's GloBE Income over the Substance-based Income Exclusion for the Investment Entity. The Top-up Tax Percentage for an Investment Entity shall be the percentage point excess, if any, of the Minimum Rate over the Effective Tax Rate of the Investment Entity. If there is more than one Investment Entity located in the jurisdiction, the MNE Group's Allocable Share of the Investment Entity's GloBE Income and the Substance-based Income Exclusion determined for each such Investment Entity are combined to compute the Effective Tax Rate of all such Investment Entities.

7.4.6. The Substance-based Income Exclusion for an Investment Entity shall be determined in accordance with the principles in Article 5.3 without regard to the exception in Article 5.3.2, and by taking into account only Eligible Tangible Assets and Eligible Payroll Costs of Eligible Employees of the Investment Entities reduced in proportion to the MNE Group's Allocable Share of the Investment Entity's GloBE Income to the Investment Entity's total GloBE Income.

Article 7.5. Investment Entity Tax Transparency Election

7.5.1. A Filing Constituent Entity may elect to treat a Constituent Entity that is an Investment Entity or an Insurance Investment Entity as a Tax Transparent Entity if the Constituent Entity-owner is subject to tax in its location under a mark-to-market or similar regime based on the annual changes in the fair value of its Ownership Interest in the Entity and the tax rate applicable to the Constituent Entity-owner with respect to such income equals or exceeds the Minimum Rate. For this purpose, a Constituent Entity that indirectly owns an Ownership Interest in an Investment Entity or Insurance Investment Entity through a direct Ownership Interest in another Investment Entity or Insurance Investment Entity is considered to be subject to tax under a mark-to-market or similar regime with respect to the indirect Ownership Interest in the first-mentioned Entity if it is subject to a mark-to-market or similar regime with respect to the direct Ownership Interest in the second-mentioned Entity.

7.5.2. The election under this Article is a Five-Year Election. If the election is revoked, gain or loss from the disposition of an asset or liability held by the Investment Entity shall be determined based on the fair value of the assets or liabilities on the first day of the revocation year.

Article 7.6. Taxable Distribution Method Election

7.6.1. At the election of the Filing Constituent Entity, a Constituent Entity-owner that is not an Investment Entity may apply the Taxable Distribution Method with respect to its Ownership Interest in a Constituent Entity that is an Investment Entity if the Constituent Entity-owner can be reasonably expected to be subject to tax on distributions from the Investment Entity at a tax rate that equals or exceeds the Minimum Rate.

7.6.2. Under the Taxable Distribution Method:

(a) distributions and deemed distributions of the Investment Entity's GloBE Income are included in the GloBE Income of the Constituent Entity-owner (other than an Investment Entity) that received the distribution;

(b) the Local Creditable Tax Gross-up is included in the GloBE Income and Adjusted Covered Taxes of the Constituent Entity-owner (other than an Investment Entity) that received the distribution;

(c) the Constituent Entity-owner's proportionate share of the Investment Entity's Undistributed Net GloBE Income for the Tested Year is treated as GloBE Income of the Investment Entity for the Reporting Fiscal Year and the result of multiplying the Minimum Rate by such GloBE Income is treated as Top-up Tax of a Low-Tax Constituent Entity in the Fiscal Year for purposes of Chapter 2; and

(d) the Investment Entity's GloBE Income or Loss for the Fiscal Year and any Adjusted Covered Taxes attributable to such income are excluded from all Effective Tax Rate computations under Chapter 5 and Articles 7.4.2 to 7.4.5, except as provided in paragraph (b).

7.6.3. The Undistributed Net GloBE Income for a Fiscal Year is the amount of the Investment Entity's GloBE Income, if any, for the Tested Year reduced (but not below zero) by:

(a) any Covered Taxes of the Investment Entity;

(b) distributions and deemed distributions to shareholders other than Constituent Entities that are Investment Entities in the Testing Period;

(c) GloBE Losses arising in the Testing Period; and

(d) Investment Loss Carry-forwards.

7.6.4. Undistributed Net GloBE Income for the Tested Year cannot be reduced by distributions or deemed distributions to the extent that such distributions were treated as a reduction to Undistributed Net GloBE Income of a previous Tested Year. For purposes of computing Undistributed Net GloBE Income, a GloBE Loss is reduced to the extent it reduced Undistributed Net GloBE Income at the end of a previous Fiscal Year. If a GloBE Loss for a Fiscal Year is not reduced to zero before the end of the end of the last Tested Period that includes such Fiscal Year, the remainder becomes an Investment Loss Carry-forward and is reduced in the same manner as a GloBE Loss in subsequent Fiscal Years.

7.6.5. For purposes of Article 7.6,

(a) the Tested Year is the third year preceding the Reporting Fiscal Year;

(b) the Testing Period is the period beginning with the first day of the Tested Year and ending with the last day of the Reporting Fiscal Year that the Ownership Interest was held by a Group Entity;

(c) a deemed distribution arises when a direct or indirect Ownership Interest in the Investment Entity is transferred to a non-Group Entity and is equal to the proportionate share of the Undistributed Net GloBE Income attributable to such Ownership Interest on the date of such transfer (determined without regard to the deemed distribution); and

(d) the Local Creditable Tax Gross-up is the amount of Covered Taxes incurred by the Investment Entity that is allowed as a credit against the Constituent Entity-owner's tax liability arising in connection with a distribution from the Investment Entity.

7.6.6. The election under this Article is a Five-Year Election. If the election is revoked, Constituent Entity-owner's proportionate share of the Investment Entity's Undistributed Net GloBE

Income for the Tested Year at the end of the Fiscal Year preceding the revocation year is treated as GloBE Income of the Investment Entity for the revocation year and the result of multiplying the Minimum Rate by such GloBE Income is treated as Top-up Tax of a Low-Tax Constituent Entity in the revocation year for purposes of Chapter 2.

8 Administration

Operation of the rules in this chapter

Chapter 8 addresses certain administrative aspects of the GloBE Rules.

- Article 8.1 sets out an MNE Groups obligation to file a standardised information return in each jurisdiction that has introduced the GloBE Rules in order to provide information on the tax calculations made by the MNE under the GloBE Rules.
- Article 8.2 allows for the development of certain safe harbours.
- Article 8.3 facilitates co-ordination between tax administrations in the application of the GloBE Rules through the development Agreed Administrative Guidance.

Article 8.1. Filing obligation

8.1.1. Subject to Article 8.1.2, each Constituent Entity located in [insert name of implementing-Jurisdiction] shall file a GloBE Information Return conforming to the requirements of Articles 8.1.4 to 8.1.6 with the tax administration of [insert name of implementing-Jurisdiction]. The return may be filed by either the Constituent Entity itself or by a Designated Local Entity on its behalf.

8.1.2. A Constituent Entity is not obligated to file a GloBE Information Return with the tax administration of [insert name of implementing-Jurisdiction] if a GloBE Information Return conforming to the requirements of Articles 8.1.4 to 8.1.6 has been filed by either:

(a) the Ultimate Parent Entity located in a jurisdiction that has a Qualifying Competent Authority Agreement in effect with [insert name of implementing-Jurisdiction] for the Reporting Fiscal Year; or

(b) the Designated Filing Entity located in a jurisdiction that has a Qualifying Competent Authority Agreement in effect with [insert name of implementing-Jurisdiction] for the Reporting Fiscal Year.

8.1.3. Where Article 8.1.2 applies, a Constituent Entity located in [insert name of implementing-Jurisdiction] or the Designated Local Entity on its behalf, shall notify the tax administration of [insert name of implementing-Jurisdiction] of the identity of the Entity that is filing the GloBE Information Return and the jurisdiction in which it is located.

8.1.4. The GloBE Information Return shall be filed in a standard template that is developed in accordance with the GloBE Implementation Framework and shall include the following information concerning the MNE Group (which shall be specified, expanded or restricted in accordance with the GloBE Implementation Framework including through the development of simplified reporting procedures):

(a) identification of the Constituent Entities, including their tax identification numbers (if they exist), the jurisdiction in which they are located and their status under the GloBE Rules,

(b) Information on the overall corporate structure of the MNE Group including the Controlling Interests in the Constituent Entities held by other Constituent Entities;

(c) the information necessary to compute:

i. the Effective Tax Rate for each jurisdiction and the Top-up Tax of each Constituent Entity under Chapter 5;

ii. the Top-up Tax of a member of the JV Group under Chapter 6;

iii. the allocation of Top-Up Tax under the IIR, and the UTPR Top-Up Tax Amount to each jurisdiction, under Chapter 2;

(d) a record of the elections made in accordance with the relevant provisions of the GloBE Rules; and

(e) other information that is agreed as part of the GloBE Implementation Framework and is necessary to carry out the administration of the GloBE Rules.

8.1.5. The GloBE Information Return shall apply the definitions and instructions contained in the standard template that is developed in accordance with the GloBE Implementation Framework.

8.1.6. The GloBE Information Return and the notifications pursuant to this Article shall be filed with the tax administration of [insert name of implementing-Jurisdiction] no later than 15 months after the last day of the Reporting Fiscal Year.

8.1.7. The tax administration of [insert name of implementing-Jurisdiction] may modify the information, filing and notification requirements of the GloBE Information Return to align those requirements with those provided under the GloBE Implementation Framework (including the development of simplified reporting procedures).

8.1.8. The laws of [insert name of implementing-Jurisdiction] with respect to penalties, sanctions and the confidentiality of returns and return information shall apply to the GloBE Information Return.

Article 8.2. Safe Harbours

8.2.1. At the election of the Filing Constituent Entity, and notwithstanding Chapter 5, the Top-up Tax for a jurisdiction (the safe harbour jurisdiction) shall be deemed to be zero for a Fiscal Year when the Constituent Entities located in this jurisdiction are eligible for a GloBE Safe Harbour, pursuant to the conditions provided under the GloBE Implementation Framework and applicable for that Fiscal Year.

8.2.2. An election made for a jurisdiction under Article 8.2.1 shall not apply in circumstances where:

(a) [insert name of implementing-Jurisdiction] could be allocated Top-up Tax under the GloBE Rules if the Effective Tax Rate for the safe harbour jurisdiction computed in accordance with Chapter 5 was below the Minimum Rate; and

(b) the tax administration of [insert name of implementing-Jurisdiction] notifies the Liable Constituent Entity (or Entities) within 36 months after the filing of the GloBE Information Return of specific facts and circumstances that may have materially affected the eligibility of the Constituent Entities located in the safe harbour jurisdiction for the relevant safe harbour and invites the Liable Constituent Entity (or Entities) to clarify within six months the effect of those facts and circumstances on the eligibility of those Constituent Entities for that safe harbour; and

(c) the Liable Constituent Entity (or Entities) fail(s) to demonstrate within the response period that those facts and circumstances did not materially affect the eligibility of the Constituent Entities for the relevant safe harbour.

Article 8.3. Administrative Guidance

8.3.1. The tax administration of [insert name of implementing-Jurisdiction] shall, subject to any requirements of domestic law, apply the GloBE Rules in accordance with any Agreed Administrative Guidance.

9 Transition rules

Operation of the rules in this chapter

Chapter 9 sets out certain Transitional Rules.

- Article 9.1 provides the transition rules that apply where an MNE Group enters within the scope of the GloBE Rules.
- Article 9.2 modifies the percentages to be applied in the calculation of the Substance-based Income Exclusion under Article 5.3 during a transitional period.
- Article 9.3 provides an exclusion from the UTPR for MNE Groups that are in the initial phase of their international activity.
- Article 9.4 provides transitional relief for filing obligations.

Article 9.1. Tax Attributes Upon Transition

9.1.1. When determining the Effective Tax Rate for a jurisdiction in a Transition Year, and for each subsequent year, the MNE Group shall take into account all of the deferred tax assets and deferred tax liabilities reflected or disclosed in the financial accounts of all of the Constituent Entities in a jurisdiction for the Transition Year. Such deferred tax assets and liabilities must be taken into account at the lower of the Minimum Rate or the applicable domestic tax rate. A deferred tax asset that has been recorded at a rate lower than the Minimum Rate may be taken into account at the Minimum Rate if the taxpayer can demonstrate that the deferred tax asset is attributable to a GloBE Loss. For purposes of applying this Article, the impact of any valuation adjustment, or accounting recognition adjustment with respect to a deferred tax asset is disregarded.

9.1.2. Deferred tax assets arising from items excluded from the computation of GloBE Income or Loss under Chapter 3 must be excluded from the Article 9.1.1 computation when such deferred tax assets are generated in a transaction that takes place after 30 November 2021.

9.1.3. In the case of a transfer of assets between Constituent Entities after 30 November 2021 and before the commencement of a Transition Year, the basis in the acquired assets (other than inventory) shall be based upon the disposing Entity's carrying value of the transferred assets upon disposition with the deferred tax assets and liabilities brought into GloBE determined on that basis.

Article 9.2. Transitional relief for the Substance-based Income Exclusion

9.2.1. For the purposes of applying Article 5.3.3, the value of 5% shall be replaced with the value set out in the table set out below for each Fiscal Year beginning in each of the following calendar years:

Fiscal Year Beginning In	Article 5.3.3 Rate
2023	10%
2024	9.8%
2025	9.6%
2026	9.4%
2027	9.2%
2028	9.0%
2029	8.2%
2030	7.4%
2031	6.6%
2032	5.8%

9.2.2. For the purposes of applying Article 5.3.4, the value of 5% shall be replaced with the value set out in the table set out below for each Fiscal Year beginning in each of the following calendar years:

Fiscal Year Beginning In	Article 5.3.4 Rate
2023	8.0%
2024	7.8%
2025	7.6%
2026	7.4%
2027	7.2%
2028	7.0%
2029	6.6%
2030	6.2%
2031	5.8%
2032	5.4%

Article 9.3. Exclusion from the UTPR of MNE Groups in the initial phase of their international activity

9.3.1. Subject to Article 9.3.4 the Top-up Tax that would otherwise be taken into account under Article 2.5.1 shall be reduced to zero during the initial phase of an MNE Group's international activity, notwithstanding the requirements otherwise provided in Chapter 5.

9.3.2. For the purposes of Article 9.3, an MNE Group is in its initial phase of its international activity if, for a Fiscal Year:

(a) it has Constituent Entities in no more than six jurisdictions; and

(b) the sum of the Net Book Values of Tangible Assets of all Constituent Entities located in all jurisdictions other than the Reference Jurisdiction does not exceed EUR 50 million.

9.3.3. For the purposes of Article 9.3.2, the Reference Jurisdiction of an MNE Group is the jurisdiction where the MNE Group has the highest total value of Tangible Assets for the Fiscal Year in which the MNE Group originally comes within the scope of the GloBE Rules. The total value of Tangible Assets in a jurisdiction is the sum of the Net Book Values of all Tangible Assets of all the Constituent Entities of the MNE Group that are located in that jurisdiction.

9.3.4. This Article 9.3 shall not apply for any Fiscal Year that starts later than five years after the first day of the first Fiscal Year when the MNE Group originally came within the scope of the GloBE Rules. For MNE Groups that are in scope of the GloBE Rules when they come into effect, the period of five years will start at the time the UTPR rules come into effect.

9.3.5. [*Optional provision*] If [insert name of implementing-Jurisdiction] is the Reference

Jurisdiction of the MNE Group pursuant to Article 9.3.3, then Article 9.3.1 shall not apply during the initial phase of that MNE Group's international activity and, during that initial phase:

(a) [*Optional provision*] the Top-up Tax calculated for a Low-Taxed Constituent Entity that would be taken into account under Article 2.5.1 shall be reduced to zero if that Low-Taxed Constituent Entity is located in the Reference Jurisdiction, notwithstanding the requirements otherwise provided in Chapter 5; and

(b) the UTPR Percentage of the jurisdictions other than the Reference Jurisdiction is deemed to be zero.

Article 9.4. Transitional relief for filing obligations

9.4.1. Notwithstanding Article 8.1.6, the GloBE Information Return or the notifications pursuant to Article 8.1 shall be filed with the tax administration of [insert name of implementing-Jurisdiction] no later than 18 months after the last day of the Reporting Fiscal Year that is the Transitional Year.

10 Definitions

> **Operation of the rules in this chapter**
>
> Chapter 10 sets out defined terms used elsewhere in the GloBE Rules.
>
> - Article 10.1 sets out general definitions that are used in the GloBE Rules.
> - Article 10.2 sets out certain definitions in respect of Flow-through Entities.
> - Article 10.3 sets out definitional rules for determining the location of an Entity for the purposes of applying the GloBE Rules.

Article 10.1. Defined Terms

10.1.1. The terms set out below have the following definitions:

Acceptable Financial Accounting Standard means International Financial Reporting Standards (IFRS) and the generally accepted accounting principles of Australia, Brazil, Canada, Member States of the European Union, Member States of the European Economic Area, Hong Kong (China), Japan, Mexico, New Zealand, the People's Republic of China, the Republic of India, the Republic of Korea, Russia, Singapore, Switzerland, the United Kingdom, and the United States of America.

Accrued Pension Expense means the difference between the amount of pension liability expense included in the Financial Accounting Net Income or Loss and the amount contributed to a Pension Fund for the Fiscal Year.

Additional Current Top-up Tax is the amount of tax determined in Article 5.4 and any amount treated as Additional Current Top-up Tax determined under Article 5.4, such as the amount determined under Article 4.1.5 or Article 7.3.

Additional Tier One Capital means an instrument issued by a Constituent Entity pursuant to prudential regulatory requirements applicable to the banking sector that is convertible to equity or written down if a pre-specified trigger event occurs and that has other features which are designed to aid loss absorbency in the event of a financial crisis.

Additions to Covered Taxes is defined in Article 4.1.2.

Adjusted Asset Gain in respect of Aggregate Asset Gain that is subject to an election under Article 3.2.6 means an amount equal to the Aggregate Asset Gain in the Election Year, reduced by any amount of such gain that has been applied against the Net Asset Loss in a prior Loss Year under Article 3.2.6(b) or (c).

Adjusted Covered Taxes is defined in Article 4.1.1.

Aggregate Asset Gain in respect of an election under Article 3.2.6, means the net gain in the Election Year from the disposition of Local Tangible Assets by all Constituent Entities located in the jurisdiction excluding the gain or loss on a transfer of assets between Group Members.

Agreed Administrative Guidance means guidance on the interpretation or administration of the GloBE Rules issued by the Inclusive Framework.

Allocable Share of the Top-up Tax is defined in Article 2.2.1.

Annual Election means an election made by a Filing Constituent Entity and that applies only for the Fiscal Year for which the election is made.

Allocated Asset Gain in respect of an election under Article 3.2.6, means the Adjusted Asset Gain that is allocated to a Fiscal Year in the Lookback Period under Article 3.2.6(d).

Arm's Length Principle means the principle under which transactions between Constituent Entities must be recorded by reference to the conditions that would have been obtained between independent enterprises in comparable transactions and under comparable circumstances.

Asymmetric Foreign Currency Gains or Losses means foreign currency gains or losses of an entity whose accounting and tax functional currencies are different and that are:

(a) included in the computation of a Constituent Entity's taxable income or loss and attributable to fluctuations in the exchange rate between its accounting functional currency and its tax functional currency;

(b) included in the computation of a Constituent Entity's Financial Accounting Net Income or Loss and attributable to fluctuations in the exchange rate between its tax functional currency and its accounting functional currency;

(c) included in the computation of a Constituent Entity's Financial Accounting Net Income or Loss and attributable to fluctuations in the exchange rate between a third foreign currency and its accounting functional currency; and

(d) attributable to fluctuations in the exchange rate between a third foreign currency and its tax functional currency, whether or not such foreign currency gain or loss is included in taxable income.

The tax functional currency is the functional currency used to determine the Constituent Entity's taxable income or loss for a Covered Tax in the jurisdiction in which it is located. The accounting functional currency is the functional currency used to determine the Constituent Entity's Financial Accounting Net Income or Loss. A third foreign currency is a currency that is not the Constituent Entity's tax functional currency or accounting functional currency.

Authorised Accounting Body is the body with legal authority in a jurisdiction to prescribe, establish, or accept accounting standards for financial reporting purposes.

Authorised Financial Accounting Standard, in respect of any Entity, means a set of generally acceptable accounting principles permitted by an Authorised Accounting Body in the jurisdiction where that Entity is located.

Average GloBE Income or Loss is defined in Article 5.5.2.

Average GloBE Revenue is defined in Article 5.5.2.

Commentary means the Commentary to the GloBE Rules as developed by the OECD/G20 Inclusive Framework on Base Erosion and Profit Shifting.

Consolidated Financial Statements means:

(a) the financial statements prepared by an Entity in accordance with an Acceptable Financial Accounting Standard, in which the assets, liabilities, income, expenses and cash flows of that Entity and the Entities in which it has a Controlling Interest are presented as those of a single economic unit;

(b) where an Entity meets the definition of a Group under Article 1.2.3, the financial statements of the Entity that are prepared in accordance with an Acceptable Financial Accounting Standard;

(c) where the Ultimate Parent Entity has financial statements described in paragraph (a) or (b) that are not prepared in accordance with an Acceptable Financial Accounting Standard, the financial statements are those that have been prepared subject to adjustments to prevent any Material Competitive Distortions; and

(d) where the Ultimate Parent Entity does not prepare financial statements described in the paragraphs above, the Consolidated Financial Statements of the Ultimate Parent Entity are those that would have been prepared if such Entity were required to prepare such statements in accordance with an Authorised Financial Accounting Standard that is either an Acceptable Financial Accounting Standard or another financial accounting standard that is adjusted to prevent any Material Competitive Distortions.

Constituent Entity (CE) is defined in Article 1.3.1.

Constituent Entity-owner means a Constituent Entity that directly or indirectly owns an Ownership Interest in another Constituent Entity of the same MNE Group.

Controlled Foreign Company Tax Regime means a set of tax rules (other than an IIR) under which a direct or indirect shareholder of a foreign entity (the controlled foreign company or CFC) is subject to current taxation on its share of part or all of the income earned by the CFC, irrespective of whether that income is distributed currently to the shareholder.

Controlling Interest means an Ownership Interest in an Entity such that the interest holder:

(a) is required to consolidate the assets, liabilities, income, expenses and cash flows of the Entity on a line-by-line basis in accordance with an Acceptable Financial Accounting Standard; or

(b) would have been required to consolidate the assets, liabilities, income, expenses and cash flows of the Entity on a line-by-line basis if the interest holder had prepared Consolidated Financial Statements.

A Main Entity is deemed to have the Controlling Interests of its Permanent Establishments.

Cooperative means an Entity that collectively markets or acquires goods or services on behalf of its members and that is subject to a tax regime in the jurisdiction in which it is located that is designed to ensure tax neutrality in respect of members' property or services sold through the cooperative and property or services acquired by members through the cooperative.

Covered Taxes is defined in Article 4.2.

Deductible Dividend means, with respect to a Constituent Entity that is subject to a Deductible Dividend Regime,

(a) a distribution of profits to the holder of an Ownership Interest that is deductible from taxable income of the Constituent Entity under the laws of the jurisdiction in which it is located; or

(b) a patronage dividend to a member of a Cooperative.

Deductible Dividend Regime means a tax regime designed to yield a single level of taxation on the owners of an Entity through a deduction from the income of the Entity for distributions of profits to the owners. For this purpose, patronage dividends of a Cooperative are treated as distributions to owners. A Deductible Dividend Regime also includes a regime applicable to Cooperatives that exempts the Cooperative from taxation.

Deemed Distribution Tax is defined in Article 7.3.2.

Deemed Distribution Tax Recapture Account means an account maintained in accordance with Article 7.3.3.

Departing Constituent Entity means a Constituent Entity that is subject to an election under Article 7.3.1 and that leaves the MNE Group or transfers substantially all of its assets to a person that is not a Constituent Entity of the same MNE Group located in the same jurisdiction.

Designated Filing Entity means the Constituent Entity, other the Ultimate Parent Entity, that has been appointed by the MNE Group to file the GloBE Information Return on behalf of the MNE Group.

Designated Local Entity means the Constituent Entity of an MNE Group that is located in [insert name of implementing-Jurisdiction] and that has been appointed by the other Constituent Entities located in [insert name of implementing-Jurisdiction] of the MNE Group to file the GloBE Information Return, or to submit the notifications under Article 8.1.3.

Disallowed Accrual is defined in Article 4.4.6.

Disposition Recapture Ratio is defined in Article 7.3.8.

Disqualified Refundable Imputation Tax means any amount of Tax, other than a Qualified Imputation Tax, accrued or paid by a Constituent Entity that is:

(a) refundable to the beneficial owner of a dividend distributed by such Constituent Entity in respect of that dividend or creditable by the beneficial owner against a tax liability other than a tax liability in respect of such dividend; or

(b) refundable to the distributing corporation upon distribution of a dividend.

Dual-listed Arrangement means an arrangement entered into by two or more Ultimate Parent Entities of separate Groups, under which:

(a) the Ultimate Parent Entities agree to combine their business by contract alone;

(b) pursuant to contractual arrangements the Ultimate Parent Entities will make distributions (with respect to dividends and in liquidation) to their shareholders based on a fixed ratio;

(c) their activities are managed as a single economic entity under contractual arrangements while retaining their separate legal identities;

(d) the Ownership Interests in the Ultimate Parent Entities comprising the agreement are quoted, traded or transferred independently in different capital markets; and

(e) the Ultimate Parent Entities prepare Consolidated Financial Statements in which the assets, liabilities, income, expenses and cash flows of all the Entities of the Groups are presented together as those of a single economic unit and that are required by a regulatory regime to be externally audited.

Effective Tax Rate (ETR) is defined in Article 5.1.1.

Election Year in respect of an Annual Election means the year for which the election is made.

Eligible Distribution Tax System means a corporate income tax system that

(a) imposes an income tax on the corporation with the tax generally payable only when the corporation distributes profits to shareholders, is deemed to distribute profits to shareholders, or incurs certain non-business expenses;

(b) imposes tax at a rate equal to or in excess of the Minimum Rate; and

(c) was in force on or before 1 July 2021.

Eligible Employees means employees, including part-time employees, of a Constituent Entity that is a member of the MNE Group and independent contractors participating in the ordinary operating activities of the MNE Group under the direction and control of the MNE Group.

Eligible Payroll Costs means employee compensation expenditures (including salaries, wages, and other expenditures that provide a direct and separate personal benefit to the employee, such as health insurance and pension contributions), payroll and employment taxes, and employer social security contributions.

Eligible Tangible Assets is defined in Article 5.3.4.

Entity means:

(a) any legal person (other than a natural person); or

(b) an arrangement that prepares separate financial accounts, such as a partnership or trust.

ETR Adjustment Article means Article 3.2.6, Article 4.4.4, Article 4.6.1, Article 4.6.4, and Article 7.3.

Excess Profit is defined in Article 5.2.2.

Excluded Dividends means dividends or other distributions received or accrued in respect of an Ownership Interest, except for:

(a) a Short-term Portfolio Shareholding, and

(b) an Ownership Interest in an Investment Entity that is subject to an election under Article 7.6.

Excluded Entity is defined in Article 1.5.1 and Article 1.5.2.

Excluded Equity Gain or Loss means the gain, profit or loss included in the Financial Accounting Net Income or Loss of the Constituent Entity arising from:

(a) gains and losses from changes in fair value of an Ownership Interest, except for a Portfolio Shareholding;

(b) profit or loss in respect of an Ownership Interest included under the equity method of accounting; and

(c) gains and losses from disposition of an Ownership Interest, except for a disposition of a Portfolio Shareholding.

Filing Constituent Entity is an Entity filing the GloBE Information Return in accordance with Article 8.1.

Financial Accounting Net Income or Loss is defined in Article 3.1.2.

Fiscal Year means an accounting period with respect to which the Ultimate Parent Entity of the MNE Group prepares its Consolidated Financial Statements. In the case of Consolidated Financial Statements as defined in paragraph (d) of its definition, Fiscal Year means the calendar year.

Five-Year Election means an election made by a Filing Constituent Entity with respect to a Fiscal Year (the election year) that cannot be revoked with respect to the election year or the four succeeding Fiscal Years. If a Five-Year Election is revoked with respect to a Fiscal Year (the revocation year), a new election cannot be made with respect to the four Fiscal Years succeeding the revocation year.

General Government means the central administration, agencies whose operations are under its effective control, state and local governments and their administrations.

GloBE Implementation Framework means the procedures to be developed by the Inclusive Framework on BEPS in order to develop administrative rules, guidance, and procedures that will facilitate the co-ordinated implementation of the GloBE Rules.

GloBE Income of all Constituent Entities is defined in Article 5.1.2(a)

GloBE Income or Loss of a Constituent Entity is defined in Article 3.1.1.

GloBE Information Return means that standardized return to be developed in accordance with the GloBE Implementation Framework that contains the information described in Article 8.1.4.

GloBE Loss Deferred Tax Asset is defined in Article 4.5.

GloBE Loss Election is defined in Article 4.5.1.

GloBE Losses of all Constituent Entities is defined in Article 5.1.2(b).

GloBE Reorganisation means a transformation or transfer of assets and liabilities such as in a merger, demerger, liquidation, or similar transaction where:

(a) the consideration for the transfer is, in whole or in significant part, equity interests issued by the acquiring Constituent Entity or by a person connected with the acquiring Constituent Entity, or, in the case of a liquidation, equity interests of the target (or, when no consideration is provided, where the issuance of an equity interest would have no economic significance);

(b) the disposing Constituent Entity's gain or loss on those assets is not subject to tax, in whole or in part; and

(c) the tax laws of the jurisdiction in which the acquiring Constituent Entity is located require the acquiring Constituent Entity to compute taxable income after the disposition or acquisition using the disposing Constituent Entity's tax basis in the assets, adjusted for any Non-qualifying Gain or Loss on the disposition or acquisition.

GloBE Revenue is defined in Article 5.5.3(a) for the purposes of Article 5.5.2.

GloBE Rules means this set of rules as developed by the OECD/G20 Inclusive Framework on Base Erosion and Profit Shifting.

GloBE Safe Harbour means the exception provided in Article 8.2.1 to facilitate compliance by MNEs and administration by tax authorities. The conditions under which the Constituent Entities of an MNE Group located in a jurisdiction are eligible to the GloBE Safe Harbour will be established in accordance with a common and agreed process to be defined as part of the work undertaken by the Inclusive Framework on BEPS to develop the GloBE Implementation Framework.

Governmental Entity means an Entity that meets all of the following criteria set out in paragraphs (a) to (d) below:

(a) it is part of or wholly-owned by a government (including any political subdivision or local authority thereof);

(b) it has the principal purpose of:

   (i) fulfilling a government function; or

   (ii) managing or investing that government's or jurisdiction's assets through the making and holding of investments, asset management, and related investment activities for the government's or jurisdiction's assets;

and does not carry on a trade or business;

(c) it is accountable to the government on its overall performance, and provides annual information reporting to the government; and

(d) its assets vest in such government upon dissolution and to the extent it distributes net earnings, such net earnings are distributed solely to such government with no portion of its net earnings inuring to the benefit of any private person.

Group is defined in Article 1.2.2 and 1.2.3.

Group Entity, in respect of any Entity or Group, means an Entity that is a member of the same Group.

High-Tax Counterparty means a Constituent Entity that is located in a jurisdiction that is not a Low-Tax Jurisdiction or that is located in a jurisdiction that would not be a Low-Tax Jurisdiction if its ETR were determined without regard to any income or expense accrued by that Entity in respect of an Intragroup Financing Arrangement.

IFRS means the International Financial Reporting Standards.

IIR means the rules set out in Article 2.1 to Article 2.3.

Included Revaluation Method Gain or Loss means the net gain or loss, increased or decreased by any associated Covered Taxes, for the Fiscal Year in respect of all property, plant and equipment that arises under an accounting method or practice that:

(a) periodically adjusts the carrying value of such property to its fair value;

(b) records the changes in value in Other Comprehensive Income; and

(c) does not subsequently report the gains or losses recorded in Other Comprehensive Income through profit and loss.

Insurance Investment Entity means an Entity that would meet the definition of an Investment Fund or a Real Estate Investment Vehicle except that it is established in relation to liabilities under an insurance or annuity contract and is wholly-owned by an Entity that is subject to regulation in its location as an insurance company.

Intermediate Parent Entity means a Constituent Entity (other than a Ultimate Parent Entity, Partially-Owned Parent Entity, Permanent Establishment, or Investment Entity) that owns (directly or indirectly) an Ownership Interest in another Constituent Entity in the same MNE Group.

International Organisation means any intergovernmental organisation (including a supranational organisation) or wholly-owned agency or instrumentality thereof that meets all of the criteria set out in paragraphs (a) to (c) below:

(a) it is comprised primarily of governments;

(b) it has in effect a headquarters or substantially similar agreement (for example, arrangements that entitle the organisation's offices or establishments in the jurisdiction (e.g. a subdivision, or a local, or regional office) to privileges and immunities) with the jurisdiction in which it is established; and

(c) law or its governing documents prevent its income inuring to the benefit of private persons.

International Shipping Income is defined in Article 3.3.2.

Intragroup Financing Arrangement means any arrangement entered into between two or more members of the MNE Group whereby a High Tax Counterparty directly or indirectly provides credit or otherwise makes an investment in a Low Tax Entity.

Investment Entity means:

(a) an Investment Fund or a Real Estate Investment Vehicle;

(b) an Entity that is at least 95% owned directly by an Entity described in paragraph (a) or through a chain of such Entities and that operates exclusively or almost exclusively to hold assets or invest funds for the benefit of such Investment Entities; and

(c) an Entity where at least 85% of the value of the Entity is owned by an Entity referred to in paragraph (a) provided that substantially all of the Entity's income is Excluded Dividends or

Excluded Equity Gain or Loss that is excluded from the computation of GloBE Income or Loss in accordance with Articles 3.2.1 (b) or (c).

Investment Fund means an Entity that meets all of the criteria set out in paragraphs (a) to (g) below:

(a) it is designed to pool assets (which may be financial and non-financial) from a number of investors (some of which are not connected);

(b) it invests in accordance with a defined investment policy;

(c) it allows investors to reduce transaction, research, and analytical costs, or to spread risk collectively;

(d) it is primarily designed to generate investment income or gains, or protection against a particular or general event or outcome;

(e) investors have a right to return from the assets of the fund or income earned on those assets, based on the contributions made by those investors;

(f) the Entity or its management is subject to a regulatory regime in the jurisdiction in which it is established or managed (including appropriate anti-money laundering and investor protection regulation); and

(g) it is managed by investment fund management professionals on behalf of the investors.

Joint Venture (JV) means an Entity whose financial results are reported under the equity method in the Consolidated Financial Statements of the Ultimate Parent Entity provided that the Ultimate Parent Entity holds directly or indirectly at least 50% of its Ownership Interests. A Joint Venture does not include:

(a) an Ultimate Parent Entity of an MNE Group that is subject to the GloBE Rules;

(b) an Excluded Entity as defined by Article 1.5.1;

(c) an Entity whose Ownership Interest held by the MNE Group are held directly through an Excluded Entity referred in Article 1.5.1 and the Entity:

   (i) operates exclusively or almost exclusively to hold assets or invest funds for the benefit of its investors;

   (ii) carries out activities that are ancillary to those carried out by the Excluded Entity; or

   (iii) substantially all of its income is excluded from the computation of GloBE Income or Loss in accordance with Articles 3.2.1(b) and (c).

(d) an Entity that is held by an MNE Group composed exclusively of Excluded Entities; or

(e) a JV Subsidiary.

JV Group means a Joint Venture and its JV Subsidiaries.

JV Group Top-up Tax means the Ultimate Parent Entity's Allocable Share of the Top-up Tax of all members of the JV Group.

JV Subsidiary means an Entity whose assets, liabilities, income, expenses and cash flows are consolidated by a Joint Venture under an Acceptable Financial Accounting Standard (or would have been required had it been required to consolidate such items in accordance with an Acceptable Financial Accounting Standard). A Permanent Establishment whose Main Entity is the Joint Venture or a JV Subsidiary shall be treated as a separate JV Subsidiary.

Liable Constituent Entity (or Entities) means one or several Constituent Entities located in [insert name of implementing-Jurisdiction] that could be liable for Top-up Tax or subject to an adjustment under Chapter 2 if the GloBE Safe Harbour in Article 8.2.1 did not apply.

Local Tangible Asset means immovable property located in the same jurisdiction as the Constituent Entity.

Look-back Period in respect of an election under Article 3.2.6, means the Election Year and the four prior Fiscal Years.

Loss Year in respect of jurisdiction for which the Filing Constituent Entity has made an election under Article 3.2.6, means a Fiscal Year in the Lookback Period for which there is a Net Asset Loss for a Constituent Entity located in that jurisdiction and the total amount of Net Asset Loss of all such Constituent Entities exceeds the total amount of their Net Asset Gain.

Low-Taxed Constituent Entity means a Constituent Entity of the MNE Group that is located in a Low-Tax Jurisdiction or a Stateless Constituent Entity that, in respect of a Fiscal Year, has GloBE Income and is subject to an Effective Tax Rate (as determined under Chapter 5) in that Fiscal Year is lower than the Minimum Rate.

Low-Tax Entity means a Constituent Entity located in a Low Tax Jurisdiction or a jurisdiction that would be a Low-Tax Jurisdiction if the Effective Tax Rate for the jurisdiction were determined without regard to any income or expense accrued by that Entity in respect of an Intragroup Financing Arrangement.

Low-Tax Jurisdiction, in respect of an MNE Group in any Fiscal Year, means a jurisdiction where the MNE Group has Net GloBE Income and is subject to an Effective Tax Rate (as determined under Chapter 5) in that period that is lower than the Minimum Rate.

Main Entity, in respect of a Permanent Establishment, is the Entity that includes the Financial Accounting Net Income or Loss of the Permanent Establishment in its financial statements.

Material Competitive Distortion in respect of the application of a specific principle or procedure under a set of generally accepted accounting principles means an application that results in an aggregate variation greater than EUR 75 million in a Fiscal Year as compared to the amount that would have been determined by applying the corresponding IFRS principle or procedure. Where the application of a specific principle or procedure results in a Material Competitive Distortion, the accounting treatment of any item or transaction subject to that principle or procedure must be adjusted to conform to the treatment required for the item or transaction under IFRS in accordance with any Agreed Administrative Guidance.

Minimum Rate means fifteen percent (15%).

Minority-Owned Constituent Entity means a Constituent Entity where the Ultimate Parent Entity has a direct or indirect Ownership Interest in that Entity of 30% or less.

Minority-Owned Parent Entity means a Minority-Owned Constituent Entity that holds, directly or indirectly, the Controlling Interests of another Minority-Owned Constituent Entity, except where the Controlling Interests of the first-mentioned Entity are held, directly or indirectly, by another Minority-Owned Constituent Entity.

Minority-Owned Subgroup means a Minority-Owned Parent Entity and its Minority-Owned Subsidiaries.

Minority-Owned Subsidiary means a Minority-Owned Constituent Entity whose Controlling Interests are held, directly or indirectly, by a Minority-Owned Parent Entity.

MNE Group is defined in Articles 1.2.1.

MNE Group's Allocable Share of the Investment Entity's GloBE Income is defined in Article 7.4.4.

Multi-Parented MNE Group means two or more Groups where:

(a) the Ultimate Parent Entities of those Groups enter into an arrangement that is a Stapled Structure or a Dual-listed Arrangement; and

(b) at least one Entity or Permanent Establishment of the combined Group is located in a different jurisdiction with respect to the location of the other Entities of the combined Group.

Net Asset Gain in respect of an election under Article 3.2.6, means the net gain from the disposition of Local Tangible Assets by a Constituent Entity located in the jurisdiction for which the election was made excluding the gain or loss on a transfer of assets to another Group Member.

Net Asset Loss in respect of a Constituent Entity and a Fiscal Year, means the net loss from the disposition of Local Tangible Assets by that Constituent Entity in that year excluding the gain or loss on a transfer of assets to another Group Member. The amount of Net Asset Loss shall be reduced by the amount of Net Asset Gain or Adjusted Asset Gain which is set-off against such loss pursuant to the application of Article 3.2.6(b) or (c) as a result of a previous election made under Article 3.2.6.

Net Book Value of Tangible Assets means the average of the beginning and end values of Tangible Assets after taking into account accumulated depreciation, depletion, and impairment, as recorded in the financial statements.

Net GloBE Income of a jurisdiction is defined in Article 5.1.2.

Net GloBE Loss of a jurisdiction is the nil or negative amount, if any, computed in accordance with the following formula:

$$Net\ GloBE\ Loss = GloBE\ Income\ of\ all\ Constituent\ Entities\ -\ GloBE\ Losses\ of\ all\ Constituent\ Entities$$

Where:

(a) the GloBE Income of all Constituent Entities is the sum of the GloBE Income of all Constituent Entities located in the jurisdiction determined in accordance with Chapter 3 for the Fiscal Year; and

(b) the GloBE Losses of all Constituent Entities is the sum of the GloBE Losses of all Constituent Entities located in the jurisdiction determined in accordance with Chapter 3 for the Fiscal Year.

Net Taxes Expense means the net amount of:

(a) any Covered Taxes accrued as an expense and any current and deferred Covered Taxes included in the income tax expense, including Covered Taxes on income that is excluded from the GloBE Income or Loss computation;

(b) any deferred tax asset attributable to a loss for the Fiscal Year;

(c) any Qualified Domestic Minimum Top-up Tax accrued as an expense;

(d) any taxes arising pursuant to the GloBE rules accrued as an expense; and

(e) any Disqualified Refundable Imputation Tax accrued as an expense.

Non-profit Organisation means an Entity that meets all of the following criteria:

(a) it is established and operated in its jurisdiction of residence:

  (i) exclusively for religious, charitable, scientific, artistic, cultural, athletic, educational, or other similar purposes; or

  (ii) as a professional organisation, business league, chamber of commerce, labour organisation, agricultural or horticultural organisation, civic league or an organisation operated exclusively for the promotion of social welfare;

(b) substantially all of the income from the activities mentioned in paragraph (a) is exempt from income tax in its jurisdiction of residence;

(c) it has no shareholders or members who have a proprietary or beneficial interest in its income or assets;

(d) the income or assets of the Entity may not be distributed to, or applied for the benefit of, a private person or non-charitable Entity other than:

  (i) pursuant to the conduct of the Entity's charitable activities;

  (ii) as payment of reasonable compensation for services rendered or for the use of property or capital; or

  (iii) as payment representing the fair market value of property which the Entity has purchased, and

(e) upon termination, liquidation or dissolution of the Entity, all of its assets must be distributed or revert to a Non-profit Organisation or to the government (including any Governmental Entity) of the Entity's jurisdiction of residence or any political subdivision thereof;

but does not include any Entity carrying on a trade or business that is not directly related to the purposes for which it was established.

Non-Qualified Refundable Tax Credit means a tax credit that is not a Qualified Refundable Tax Credit but that is refundable in whole or in part.

Non-qualifying Gain or Loss means the lesser of the gain or loss of the disposing Constituent Entity arising in connection with a GloBE Reorganisation that is subject to tax in the disposing Constituent Entity's location and the financial accounting gain or loss arising in connection with the GloBE Reorganisation.

Number of Employees, for the purposes of the UTPR percentage, means the total number of employees on a full-time equivalent (FTE) basis of all the Constituent Entities resident for tax purposes in the relevant tax jurisdiction. For this purpose, independent contractors participating in the ordinary operating activities of the Constituent Entity are reported as employees. With regard to Permanent Establishments, employees should be allocated to the tax jurisdiction in which the Permanent Establishment is located when the payroll costs of such employees are included in the separate financial accounts of that Permanent Establishment as determined by Article 3.4.1 and adjusted in accordance with 3.4.2. The Number of Employees attributed to the tax jurisdiction of a Permanent Establishment shall not be taken into account for the Number of Employees of the tax jurisdiction of the Main Entity.

OECD Model Tax Convention means the OECD (2017), Model Tax Convention on Income and on Capital: Condensed Version 2017, OECD Publishing, Paris, https://doi.org/10.1787/mtc_cond-2017-en.

Other Comprehensive Income means items of income and expense that are not recognised in profit or loss as required or permitted by the Authorised Financial Accounting Standard used in the Consolidated Financial Statements. Other Comprehensive Income is usually reported as an adjustment to equity in the statement of financial position (balance sheet).

Ownership Interest means any equity interest that carries rights to the profits, capital or reserves of an Entity, including the profits, capital or reserves of a Main Entity's Permanent Establishment(s).

Parent Entity means an Ultimate Parent Entity that is not an Excluded Entity, an Intermediate Parent Entity, or a Partially-Owned Parent Entity.

Parent Entity's Inclusion Ratio is defined in Article 2.2.2.

Partially-Owned Parent Entity means a Constituent Entity (other than a Ultimate Parent Entity, Permanent Establishment, or Investment Entity) that:

(a) owns (directly or indirectly) an Ownership Interest in another Constituent Entity of the same MNE Group; and

(b) has more than 20% of the Ownership Interests in its profits held directly or indirectly by persons that are not Constituent Entities of the MNE Group.

Passive Income means income included in GloBE Income that is:

(a) a dividend or dividend equivalents;

(b) interest or interest equivalent;

(c) rent;

(d) royalty;

(e) annuity; or

(f) net gains from property of a type that produces income described in paragraphs (a) to (e),

but only to the extent a Constituent Entity-owner is subject to tax on such income under a Controlled Foreign Company Tax Regime or as a result of an Ownership Interest in a Hybrid Entity.

Pension Fund means:

(a) an Entity that is established and operated in a jurisdiction exclusively or almost exclusively to administer or provide retirement benefits and ancillary or incidental benefits to individuals:

i. regulated as such by that jurisdiction or one of its political subdivisions or local authorities; or

ii. those benefits are secured or otherwise protected by national regulations and funded by a pool of assets held through a fiduciary arrangement or trustor to secure the fulfilment of the corresponding pension obligations against a case of insolvency of the MNE Group; and

(b) a Pension Services Entity.

Pension Services Entity means an Entity that is established and operated exclusively or almost exclusively:

(a) to invest funds for the benefit of Entities referred to in paragraph (a) of the definition of Pension Fund; or

(b) to carry out activities that are ancillary to those regulated activities carried out by the Entities referred to in paragraph (a) of the definition of Pension Fund provided that they are members of the same Group.

Permanent Establishment means:

(a) a place of business (including a deemed place of business) situated in a jurisdiction and treated as a permanent establishment in accordance with an applicable Tax Treaty in force provided that such jurisdiction taxes the income attributable to it in accordance with a provision similar to Article 7 of the OECD Model Tax Convention on Income and on Capital;

(b) if there is no applicable Tax Treaty in force, a place of business (including a deemed place of business) in respect of which a jurisdiction taxes under its domestic law the income attributable to such place of business on a net basis similar to the manner in which it taxes its own tax residents;

(c) if a jurisdiction has no corporate income tax system, a place of business (including a deemed place of business) situated in that jurisdiction that would be treated as a permanent establishment in accordance with the OECD Model Tax Convention on Income and on Capital provided that such jurisdiction would have had the right to tax the income attributable to it in accordance with Article 7 of that model; or

(d) a place of business (or a deemed place of business) that is not already described in paragraphs (a) to (c) through which operations are conducted outside the jurisdiction where the Entity is located provided that such jurisdiction exempts the income attributable to such operations.

Policy Disallowed Expenses means:

(a) expenses accrued by the Constituent Entity for illegal payments, including bribes and kickbacks; and

(b) expenses accrued by the Constituent Entity for fines and penalties that equal or exceed EUR 50 000 (or an equivalent in the functional currency in which the Constituent Entity's Financial Accounting Net Income or Loss was calculated).

Portfolio Shareholding means Ownership Interests in an Entity that are held by the MNE Group and that carry rights to less than 10% of the profits, capital, reserves, or voting rights of that Entity at the date of the distribution or disposition.

Prior Period Errors and Changes in Accounting Principles means all changes in the opening equity at the beginning of the Fiscal Year of a Constituent Entity attributable to:

(a) a correction of an error in the determination of Financial Accounting Net Income in a previous Fiscal Year that affected the income or expenses includible in the computation of GloBE Income or Loss for such Fiscal Year, except to the extent such error correction resulted in a material decrease to a liability for Covered Taxes subject to Article 4.6; or

(b) a change in accounting principle or policy that affects income or expenses includible in the computation of GloBE Income or Loss.

Qualified Ancillary International Shipping Income is defined in Article 3.3.3.

Qualified Domestic Minimum Top-up Tax means a minimum tax that is included in the domestic law of a jurisdiction and that:

(a) determines the Excess Profits of the Constituent Entities located in the jurisdiction (domestic Excess Profits) in a manner that is equivalent to the GloBE Rules;

(b) operates to increase domestic tax liability with respect to domestic Excess Profits to the Minimum Rate for the jurisdiction and Constituent Entities for a Fiscal Year; and

(c) is implemented and administered in a way that is consistent with the outcomes provided for under the GloBE Rules and the Commentary, provided that such jurisdiction does not provide any benefits that are related to such rules.

A Qualified Domestic Minimum Top-up Tax may compute domestic Excess Profits based on an Acceptable Financial Accounting Standard permitted by the Authorised Accounting Body or an Authorised Financial Accounting Standard adjusted to prevent any Material Competitive Distortions, rather than the financial accounting standard used in the Consolidated Financial Statements.

Qualified IIR means a set of rules equivalent to Article 2.1 to Article 2.3 of the GloBE Rules (including any provisions of the GloBE Rules associated with those articles) that are included in the domestic law of a jurisdiction and that are implemented and administered in a way that is consistent with the outcomes provided for under the GloBE Rules and the Commentary provided that such jurisdiction does not provide any benefits that are related to such rules.

Qualified Imputation Tax means a Covered Tax accrued or paid by a Constituent Entity that is refundable or creditable to the beneficial owner of a dividend distributed by such Constituent Entity (or, in the case of a Covered Tax accrued or paid by a Permanent Establishment, a dividend distributed by the Main Entity) to the extent that the refund is payable, or the credit is provided:

(a) by a jurisdiction other than the jurisdiction which imposed the Covered Taxes under a foreign tax credit regime;

(b) to a beneficial owner of the dividend that is subject to tax at a nominal rate that equals or exceeds the Minimum Rate on the dividend on a current basis under the domestic law of the jurisdiction which imposed the Covered Taxes on the Constituent Entity;

(c) to an individual beneficial owner of the dividend who is tax resident in the jurisdiction which imposed the Covered Taxes on the Constituent Entity and who is subject to tax on the dividends as ordinary income; or

(d) to a Governmental Entity, an International Organisation, a resident Non-profit Organisation, a resident Pension Fund, a resident Investment Entity that is not a Group Entity, or a resident life insurance company to the extent that the dividends are received in connection with a pension fund business and subject to tax in a similar manner as a dividend received by Pension Fund.

For purposes of paragraph (d), a Non-Profit Organisation or Pension Fund is resident in a jurisdiction if it is created and managed in that jurisdiction, and an Investment Entity is resident in a jurisdiction if it is created and regulated in the jurisdiction. A life insurance company is resident in the jurisdiction in which it is located.

Qualified Refundable Tax Credit means a refundable tax credit designed in a way such that it must be paid as cash or available as cash equivalents within four years from when a Constituent Entity satisfies the conditions for receiving the credit under the laws of the jurisdiction granting the credit. A tax credit that is refundable in part is a Qualified Refundable Tax Credit to the extent it must be paid as cash or available as cash equivalents within four years from when a Constituent Entity satisfies the conditions for receiving the credit under the laws of the jurisdiction granting the credit. A Qualified Refundable Tax Credit does not include any amount of tax creditable or refundable pursuant to a Qualified Imputation Tax or a Disqualified Refundable Imputation Tax.

Qualified UTPR means a set of rules equivalent to Article 2.4 to Article 2.6 of the GloBE Rules (including any provisions of the GloBE Rules associated with those articles) that are included in the domestic law of a jurisdiction and that are implemented and administered in a way that is consistent with the outcomes provided for under the GloBE Rules and the Commentary provided that such jurisdiction does not provide any benefits that are related to such rules.

Qualifying Competent Authority Agreement means a bilateral or multilateral agreement or arrangement between Competent Authorities that provides for the automatic exchange of annual GloBE Information Returns.

Real Estate Investment Vehicle means an Entity the taxation of which achieves a single level of taxation either in its hands or the hands of its interest holders (with at most one year of deferral), provided that that person holds predominantly immovable property and is itself widely held.

Recaptured Deferred Tax Liability is defined in Article 4.4.4.

Recapture Exception Accrual is defined in Article 4.4.5.

Reductions to Covered Taxes is defined in Article 4.1.3.

Reference Jurisdiction is defined in Article 9.3.3.

Reporting Fiscal Year means the Fiscal Year that is the subject of the GloBE Information Return.

Short-term Portfolio Shareholding means a Portfolio Shareholding that has been economically held by the Constituent Entity that receives or accrues the dividends or other distributions for less than one year at the date of the distribution.

Stapled Structure means an arrangement entered into by two or more Ultimate Parent Entities of separate Groups, under which:

(a) 50% or more of the Ownership Interests in the Ultimate Parent Entities of the separate Groups are by reason of form of ownership, restrictions on transfer, or other terms or conditions combined with each other, and cannot be transferred or traded independently. If the combined Ownership Interests are listed, they are quoted at a single price; and

(b) one of those Ultimate Parent Entities prepares Consolidated Financial Statements in which the assets, liabilities, income, expenses and cash flows of all the Entities of the Groups are presented together as those of a single economic unit and that are required by a regulatory regime to be externally audited.

Stateless Constituent Entity means a Constituent Entity described in Article 10.3.2(b) and Article 10.3.3(d).

Substance-based Income Exclusion is defined in Article 5.3.

Tangible Assets, for the purposes of the UTPR percentage and for Article 9.3, means the Tangible Assets of all the Constituent Entities resident for tax purposes in the relevant tax jurisdiction. Tangible Assets do not include cash or cash equivalents, intangibles, or financial assets. With regard to Permanent Establishments, Tangible Assets should be allocated to the tax jurisdiction in which the Permanent Establishment is located provided those Tangible Assets are included in the separate financial accounts of that Permanent Establishment as determined by Article 3.4.1 and adjusted in accordance with Article 3.4.2. The Tangible Assets allocated to the tax jurisdiction of a Permanent Establishment shall not be taken into account for the Tangible Assets of the tax jurisdiction of the Main Entity.

Tax means a compulsory unrequited payment to General Government.

Taxable Distribution Method is defined in Article 7.6.2.

Tax Treaty means an agreement for the avoidance of double taxation with respect to taxes on income and on capital.

Tested Year is defined in Article 7.6.5.

Testing Period is defined in Article 7.6.5.

Top-up Tax means the top-up tax computed for the jurisdiction or Constituent Entity pursuant to Article 5.2.

Top-up Tax Percentage is defined in Article 5.2.1.

Total Deferred Tax Adjustment Amount is defined in Article 4.4.1.

Total UTPR Top-up Tax Amount means the total amount of Top-up Tax that is allocable under the UTPR as defined in Article 2.4.1.

Transition Year, for a jurisdiction, means the first Fiscal Year that the MNE Group comes within the scope of the GloBE Rules in respect of that jurisdiction.

Ultimate Parent Entity (UPE) is defined in Article 1.4.

Undistributed Net GloBE Income is defined in Article 7.6.3.

UPE Jurisdiction means the jurisdiction where the Ultimate Parent Entity is located.

UTPR means the rules set out in Article 2.4 to Article 2.6.

UTPR Jurisdiction means a jurisdiction that has a Qualified UTPR in force.

UTPR Percentage means the percentage of Total UTPR Top-up Tax Amount that is allocated to a UTPR Jurisdiction in accordance with the formula provided in 2.6.1.

UTPR Top-up Tax Amount means the amount of Top-up Tax allocated to a UTPR Jurisdiction under the UTPR.

Article 10.2. Definitions of Flow-through Entity, Tax Transparent Entity, Reverse Hybrid Entity, and Hybrid Entity

10.2.1. An Entity is a **Flow-through Entity** to the extent it is fiscally transparent with respect to its income, expenditure, profit or loss in the jurisdiction where it was created unless it is tax resident and subject to a Covered Tax on its income or profit in another jurisdiction.

(a) A Flow-Through Entity is a **Tax Transparent Entity** with respect to its income, expenditure, profit or loss to the extent that it is fiscally transparent in the jurisdiction in which its owner is located.

(b) A Flow-Through Entity is a **Reverse Hybrid Entity** with respect to its income, expenditure, profit or loss to the extent that it is not fiscally transparent in the jurisdiction in which the owner is located.

10.2.2. An Entity is treated as fiscally transparent under the laws of a jurisdiction, if that jurisdiction treats the income, expenditure, profit or loss of that Entity as if it were derived or incurred by the direct owner of that Entity in proportion to its interest in that Entity.

10.2.3. An Ownership Interest in an Entity or a Permanent Establishment that is a Constituent Entity shall be treated as held through a **Tax Transparent Structure** if that Ownership Interest is held indirectly through a chain of Tax Transparent Entities.

10.2.4. A Constituent Entity that is not a tax resident and not subject to a Covered Tax or a Qualified Domestic Minimum Top-up Tax based on its place of management, place of creation, or similar criteria shall be treated as a Flow-Through Entity and a Tax Transparent Entity in respect of its income, expenditure, profit or loss to the extent that:

(a) its owners are located in a jurisdiction that treats the Entity as fiscally transparent;

(b) it does not have a place of business in the jurisdiction where it was created; and

(c) the income, expenditure, profit or loss is not attributable to a Permanent Establishment.

10.2.5. An Entity that is treated as a separate taxable person for income tax purposes in the jurisdiction where it is located is a **Hybrid Entity** with respect to its income, expenditure, profit or loss to the extent that it is fiscally transparent in the jurisdiction in which its owner is located.

Article 10.3. Location of an Entity and a Permanent Establishment

10.3.1. The location of an Entity that is not a Flow-through Entity is determined as follows:

(a) if it is a tax resident in a jurisdiction based on its place of management, place of creation or similar criteria, it is located in that jurisdiction; and

(b) in other cases, it is located in the jurisdiction in which it was created.

10.3.2. The location of an Entity that is a Flow-through Entity is determined as follows:

(a) if it is the Ultimate Parent Entity of the MNE Group or it is required to apply an IIR in accordance with Article 2.1, it is located in the jurisdiction where it was created; and

(b) in other cases, it shall be treated as a stateless Entity.

10.3.3. The location of a Permanent Establishment is determined as follows:

(a) if it is described in paragraph (a) of the definition in Article 10.1, is located in the jurisdiction where it is treated as a permanent establishment and is taxed under the applicable Tax Treaty in force;

(b) if it is described in paragraph (b) of the definition in Article 10.1, is located in the jurisdiction where it is subject to net basis taxation based on its business presence;

(c) if it is described in paragraph (c) of the definition in Article 10.1, is located in the jurisdiction where it is situated; and

(d) if it is described in paragraph (d) of the definition in Article 10.1, is considered as a stateless Permanent Establishment.

10.3.4. Where by reason of Article 10.3.1, a Constituent Entity is located in more than one jurisdiction (a dual-located Entity), then its status for purposes of the GloBE Rules shall be determined as follows:

(a) if it is located in two jurisdictions that have an applicable Tax Treaty in force:

(i) it shall be located in the jurisdiction where it is considered as a deemed resident for purposes of the Tax Treaty;

(ii) if the Tax Treaty requires the competent authorities to reach a mutual agreement on the deemed residence of the Constituent Entity for purposes of the Tax Treaty and no agreement exists, then paragraph (b) shall apply;

(iii) if the Tax Treaty does not provide relief or exemption from tax because the Constituent Entity is a tax resident of both Contracting Parties, then paragraph (b) shall apply;

(b) if no Tax Treaty applies, then its location shall be determined as follows:

(i) it shall be located in the jurisdiction where it paid the greater amount of Covered Taxes for the Fiscal Year, without considering the ones paid in accordance with a Controlled Foreign Company Tax Regime;

(ii) if the amount of Covered Taxes paid in both jurisdiction is the same or zero, it shall be located in the jurisdiction where it has the greater amount of Substance-based Income Exclusion computed on an entity basis in accordance with Article 5.3;

(iii) if the amount of the Substance-based Income Exclusion in both jurisdictions is the same or zero, then it is considered a Stateless Constituent Entity unless it is the Ultimate Parent Entity of the MNE Group in which case it shall be located in the jurisdiction where it was created.

10.3.5. Where, under Article 10.3.4, a dual-located Entity that is a Parent Entity is located in a jurisdiction where it is not subject to a Qualified IIR, then the other jurisdiction can require such Entity to apply its Qualified IIR unless it is restricted by an applicable Tax Treaty in force.

10.3.6. Where an Entity has changed its location during the Fiscal Year, it shall be located in the jurisdiction where it was located at the beginning of that year.

www.ingramcontent.com/pod-product-compliance
Ingram Content Group UK Ltd.
Pitfield, Milton Keynes, MK11 3LW, UK
UKHW051507290926
15471UKWH00008B/1481

9 789264 727731